Number Two
Studies in Architecture and Culture

**Books are to be returned on or before
the last date below.**

LIBREX —

Urban Forms, Suburban Dreams

Edited by Malcolm Quantrill and Bruce Webb

Texas A&M University Press, College Station

This series was initiated with the support of the Graham Foundation
for Advanced Studies in the Fine Arts, Chicago.

The paper used in this book meets the minimum requirements
of the American National Standard for Permanence of Paper
for Printed Library Materials, Z39.48-1984.
Binding materials have been chosen for durability.

Library of Congress Cataloging-in-Publication Data

Urban forms, suburban dreams / edited by Malcolm Quantrill and Bruce
    Webb.
            p.   cm. — (Studies in architecture and culture ; 2)
        ISBN 0-89096-535-8
        1. Suburban homes—United States.   2. Architecture, Modern—20th
    century—United States.   3. Suburban homes—Europe.
    4. Architecture, Modern—20th century—Europe.   I. Quantrill,
    Malcolm, 1931–   .   II. Webb, Bruce, 1941–   .   III. Series.
    NA7571.U73   1993
    728′.09′04—dc20   92-43269
                                                                 CIP

To Antero Markelin,
professor of urban and regional planning
at the University of Stuttgart,
in celebration of his sixtieth birthday

Contents

Illustrations

Preface

The Center for the Advancement of Studies in Architecture (CASA) international symposium that generated this second volume of our "Studies in Architecture and Culture" was held in Texas in October, 1990, at The Woodlands, a planned community twenty miles north of Houston. Indeed, The Woodlands has a perfect correspondence with the theme of this second CASA meeting, "Places between Here and There." In characteristic fashion, Peter Eisenman objected to such a concept of location (or nonlocation) theory, protesting: "There just isn't any here and there any more." Yet surely this caveat reflects and supports our notion that, for many, the present sense of place is "neither here nor there." For our intention in focusing on the *between* was literally to explore the *Zwischenraum* sandwiched between urbs and urbs (or, for that matter, between sub-urbs and sub-urbs).

Eisenman's contribution here, under the heading of "Architecture in a Mediated Environment," proposes that all distinctions between here and there have been dissolved by the ubiquitous presence of the media—that is to say, one medium, tele-video. What Eisenman wants us to believe is that the verb "to mediate" means "to influence or to affect by the use of media"—whereas we know that to mediate means to occupy a middle position, allowing one (it) to act as an intermediary and, consequently, to mediate. Architecture is itself a mediator; or, as Norberg-Schulz has pointed out, it is "an intermediary object." Perhaps Eisenman is proposing that the tele-video screen is displacing architecture as the intermediary object? Is he also suggesting that architecture give up its middle ground of *commoditas,* abandon its essential *firmitas,* and forsake the generation of an earthly *venustas* to become instead merely a cover girl—*una donna audace?*

Colin Rowe's "Present Urban Predicament" is of another order entirely. This contribution dates from the late 1970s and parallels the book *Collage City* that Rowe wrote with Fred Koetter. In Rowe's collage process the historical bodies of the city are dissected, offering specimen organs and joints that can be reconstructed into new assemblages. This allows each piece of architecture to fulfill the role of mediating between its neighbors, an intermediary object that plays glove, mirror and speculum—fitting an outstretched urban hand; reflecting profiles, junctions and entrances; and opening up unexplored interstices of the city's anatomy. This three-dimensional jigsaw, permitting the invention of urban form by reference to well-known parts of cities, is advanced as a history-based theory that offers an antidote for sterile modernist formula-planning. According to modernist theories of the 1920s and '30s, each rampant tower of rib roast was flattened to become mere Frankfurter. Rowe believes that the "collage city" of contrasts and complexities would replace the sausage texture of the Frankfurter with the variety of a *Karjalaanpaistia* (the Karelian casserole of mixed meats).

Kaisa Broner-Bauer's account of the modernist city as a lost utopia poignantly and accurately places the misplaced social idealism of the modern movement in the context of its nineteenth-century precursors. The utopian principles of post-Enlightenment planned communities are traced from Saltaire through Robert Owen and Pullman to Ebenezer Howard's "garden city," Garnier's *cité indus-trielle* and Le Corbusier's *ville radieuse.* Somewhere between social engineering, diagrammatics, and certain geometric dispositions lay the perfect order for both urbs and sub-urbs, and the search for this elusive utopia occupied many minds and drawing boards. Perfect villages such as Bedford Park and Port Sunlight were created for *perfect* owners or "controlled" tenants. The Woodlands, Texas, continues this pursuit in the late twentieth century with a residual focus on the American Dream. This dream, which is predicated on the basis of "paradise without taxes," remains, as the warning signs in The Woodlands and the symposium chairman reminded us, "SLIPPERY WHEN WET." Between urban forms and suburban dreams lie many slippery paths, and we have trodden most of them in search of these lost utopias.

Broner-Bauer, while not entirely on the side of modernist strategies, rightly defends attempts to make the romance of past cul-de-sac solutions into hygienic and habitable environments. The fact that those strategies led to repetition (without apparent Georgian virtues!), boredom and (sometimes) a *nouveau-malpropreté,* does not invalidate the moral intent of those who sought within the tradition of utopian principles and fervor to substitute a uniform standard of light and hygiene for the accumulated darkness and squalor of historical accident. Surely with modernist enlightenment, constructional and sanitary techniques, plus the advantages of progressive and scientific planning, it was impossible not to succeed. What happened, then, to our Brave New World? It seems that we are barely aware of the appropriate questions, let alone satisfactory answers.

Nevertheless, as Dennis Domer admirably demonstrates, under President Franklin Delano Roosevelt's New Deal, the entrepreneur developer Gustave Ring built astonishingly successful suburban villages in Virginia just across the Potomac River from Washington, D.C. Now, more than half a century later, the apartments in these villages are more than ever in demand as desirable homes for those working in the nation's capital. In the example of Arlington Village, we see the persistence of Howard's garden city. Arlington Village represents a fragment of the garden city cast into the suburban wilderness: at once a dormitory community and a thoughtfully landscaped semirural village that ingenuously denies its apartment basis by the skilful adaptation of scaled-down English village terraced housing. And if we ask why such housing has been and remains popular, the answer might perhaps be that the concept, realization, and appreciation of such "places between here and there" as Arlington Village and The Woodlands is not mediated by the *haute-couture* of fashion magazine covers. Eisenman may purvey his "emperor's new clothes," but their transparency is not merely literal — it is truly phenomenal.

A contrasting scale and purpose is addressed in Marco Frascari's "A Wonder of the *City Beautiful* Suburbia: the *Mirabilis Suburbis* of Coral Gables, Miami." Frascari exhibits here a truly Italian passion. For what disappoints him in so much aspirant architecture of today is not that it lacks scale, proportion, technical mastery, or ingenious manipulation of form and surface, *but that it fails to generate a sense of wonder in the beholder.* And Frascari does not mean: "Haha, I wonder what he's up to?" He is concerned, rather, with the miraculous, the astonishing, the astounding, a revelation of a world beyond the reality and commonplace of everyday existence. In Frascari's sense the role of architecture is to fill that *Zwischenraum* between our uncultivated present and the prospect of the promised garden of paradise. This endows architecture with a deep responsibility, a spiritual obligation that cannot be fulfilled by mere technical dexterity or conjuring with words and geometric puzzles.

The Persian word for garden is *faradis,* from which we derive our notion of paradise as a green and luxuriant oasis that offers respite from the cruel and harsh desert. It is a refuge of joy after the pain and torment of this world, a garden of delight in which even the Muslims believe there will be drinking and dancing. And it is this *venustas,* a sense of delight, that Frascari is seeking with his quest for wonder in architecture. We find it in Van Gogh's paintings, and in those of Gauguin and Cézanne; it is in Duchamp's "Nude Descending a Staircase" and "A Bride Surrounded by Her Bachelors." It is there, too, in Frank Lloyd Wright's Unity Temple, his dendriform columns of the Johnson Wax Building, and the interior of the Solomon Guggenheim Museum. Piranesi captured it in his *carceri* drawings, as does the fantastic architecture proposed by Lebbeus Woods. Frascari has discovered it in the eclectic vignettes of Coral Gables, Miami, where the various hybrids of Chinese, French, Italian, and Spanish architecture are planted as superpostcard scale memories of Granada, Normandy, Peking, and Venice.

In the light shed by these reflections on the *mirabilis suburbis* of Coral Gables, the prospects for a new town on Florida's west coast that rejoices in the name

Seaside would seem bright and promising. With memories of the ocean lapping on the shore, the echoes of laughter and shouts from ball games on the beach still fresh in our ears, and our astonishment at the gaiety—almost raucousness—of form and color delineated by the carpenter's witty variations on nautical themes fuelling our expectations, we eagerly await the inventions of architects Duany and Plater-Zyberk.

Alas, as Drexel Turner relates, the road to paradise, like that to hell, is paved with good intentions. The major sin, it appears, in the case of Duany and Plater-Zyberk (aided and abetted by Leon Krier) is their mistaken belief that the key to the attainment of paradise is to have as many rules as possible for good behavior. Yet one cannot imagine, considering Duany's naive misinterpretation of Alvar Aalto's sense of form and fun, or Krier's constipated view of town planning (albeit one that endears him to Charles, Prince of Wales), that any explosion of the *bon-vivant* and the smack of vulgarity (acknowledged from the time of the Prince Regent to that of Edward VII as being essential to any buildings or goings-on associated with the seaside) could be generated by this unlikely marriage of talents and prospects.

We have known since the era of the bathing machine that the principal function of the seaside experience is escape from one's inhibitions. It is necessary to let (at least) your hair down. Bouncing and flopping about on the ocean's edge requires an exuberant architecture of accommodation, buildings that reflect waves of water and laughter in their forms and details. It is at the seaside that we shed our skins of infancy and puberty and grow up. But Seaside, according to Duany, Plater-Zyberk, and Krier, is still confined to the Victorian nursery-kindergarten regime. Frank Lloyd Wright, as Grant Manson told us, was initiated into the wonder of architectural form by playing with Frobel blocks, *not through early toilet-training*. Certainly the Edwardians (and probably the Victorians, too) had more fun at the seaside than Duany, Plater-Zyberk, and Krier will allow us. If only Duany really believed in his Aalto "heads and tails" theory, he might have given birth to a gentle, friendly monster, a leviathan, perhaps, that would spurt a little life and levity into Seaside, relieving its determination to be a holiday camp for time-sharing puritans. Sadly, puritans never seem to get the point of paradise, which is: There's no point in praying for the good life, unless you actually believe in it.

Of course, if you can't afford the good life, or you wish to avoid the dangers to life and limb—not to speak of the hazards of foreign food attached to traveling abroad—then you can settle for an American-built, home-cooked *tranche-de-vie* in Florida's Disney World. By extravagant ingenuity, Disney World, Florida, manages to roll urbs and sub-urbs into one. For example, the endless bypass that you have to take in order to get anywhere ensures that you are always somewhere "between here and there." In the distance, on the horizon, we are constantly aware of the promised land. But, in conformity with the promise of Houston's skyline, when we arrive downtown we discover "there is no there there!" That's the Disney magic. When we are between here and there, we can see there clearly—for example the superscale of the Dolphin and Swan hotels. But this gigantic promise fades on arrival, proving that you cannot make a big-city block in the middle of nowhere. If we were to guess at the master mind behind Disney World (since nobody will own up), then it would be Hans Hollein. Recalling his city image of the aircraft carrier parked in the landscape, we might also remember Lord Nelson's determination at Trafalgar. Clapping his telescope to his blind eye, and scouring the ocean, Nelson pronounced: "I see no ships." So it is with Disney World. And there, at Orlando, in the middle of nowhere, it's fun to remember how much more fun it is to be somewhere. And that's very interesting, because quite clearly (in Eisenman's terms) the people responsible for Disney World have instructed Messrs. Michael Graves, Robert Stern, and Arato Isozaki to fabricate a mediated environment. If they have succeeded (and financially they certainly have), then we may well have a basis for distinguishing between architecture and the ubiquitous cover girl, *la donna audace*. Sadly, Disney World is a parasitic environment, living off memories that don't exist and are only feebly suggested. There is no wonder there either.

Malcolm Quantrill
Bruce Webb

Acknowledgments

The editors would like to recognize the support of the following individuals and organizations in the preparation of this second volume of the Studies in Architecture and Culture series.

Thanks must go first of all to George P. Mitchell, chief executive officer of Mitchell Energy and Development Corporation, whose personal enthusiasm and generous support made possible the symposium at The Woodlands, Texas, in October, 1990, on the suburban theme "Places between Here and There." Deborah Hartmann, then of Dancie Perugini Ware, was extremely energetic in promoting the collaboration between Mr. Mitchell and CASA, and we also had extensive collaboration from The Woodlands Corporation.

In addition, two of the lectures were sponsored by Dr. Wilem W. Frischmann of Pell Frischmann, Engineers, London, and the architectural office of Sheppard Robson and Partners, London. Continued funding came from host institutions— Texas A&M University through the College of Architecture, and the University of Houston through the Brochstein Foundation's endowment to their College of Architecture. Further endorsement of this publishing venture came in the form of a grant from the Thomas Cubitt Trust of London for each of the first two volumes of the series.

We are indebted to a number of other individuals. Raymond Brochstein's support of the College of Architecture at the University of Houston makes continuing publication possible. Edwin Eubanks of the Anchorage Foundation facilitated additional support from that organization. Peter Wood, interim dean of the College of Architecture, University of Houston, 1990–92, gave his unfaltering endorsement to this project in the wake of Dean Bill Jenkins's untimely death. Francelle Harris, Professor Quantrill's assistant, 1990–91, was responsible for the preparation of the final manuscript, while the staff at the Texas A&M University Press watched over its progress towards production. We must also mention the contribution by Ken Garland of London for the design concept that guided our original formulation of the first volume; this mention was unfortunately omitted from the first volume.

For architects, not unnaturally, it is the actual graphic design and layout that adds the important final touch to the product. To ensure that we would be able to establish and satisfy high standards in regard to the feel and appearance of these books, the Graham Foundation for Advanced Studies in the Fine Arts made a grant available in 1989. We therefore wish to record our gratitude to the Graham Foundation for the early encouragement that has made it possible to realize our original goals.

Urban Forms, Suburban Dreams

Number Two
Studies in Architecture and Culture

Architecture in a Mediated Environment

Peter Eisenman

The subtitle of this symposium—"Places between Here and There"—is, I believe, the wrong one for our situation today because we are not talking about places, but about events. In a media environment there are no longer places in the sense that we used to know them; but purpose. The dialectic "here and there" is no longer adequate to describe the conditions of a media event, nor of a condition of between.

What is meant by present-day reality? Architecture and urbanism used to define reality. The notions of place-making, of here-and-there, of house and home, of bricks and mortar—all of these terms defined, for most of us, what reality was. But today that reality has changed and we are no longer able to understand these terms in quite the same way.

Prior to 1945, I think that in the so-called modernist world, it was clear what reality was—what a city was, and what a place was. This was because there was such a thing as an object and objectives. It was thought philosophically that the concept of "object" could be understood. Heidegger went so far as to say there was such a thing as a *being in the thing,* or a "being in the object." Heidegger's idea of this beingness of objects defines the first half of the twentieth-century view of the object.

After 1960, there emerged a group loosely called poststructuralists or postobjectists, part of what we know broadly as Postmodernism. These people said reality was a matter of interpretation and a matter of language. For example, Fredric Jameson's book, *The Prison House of Language,* dealt with the notion that everything was a question of interpretation; that we were caught not in the being of the thing, but in the prison house of interpretation.

Now, interpretation is really a question of values; therefore, we could say that we have moved from a world of facts to a world of values. F. R. S. Northrop once said, "Facts are like sacks. If you do not put anything in them, they refuse to stand up." Today then, there is a world of objects that are full of interpretation. Poststructuralism said that every object was a sign and that every sign dealt with a question of interpretation. Thus, the dominant ethos of the last thirty years is one of customization, until moronism's strange realization occurred. This was presented by the world of media.

Media deal neither with facts nor with interpretation, but with the cool, autonomous condition (or supposedly so) of reproduction. We can think of the Xerox machine, the telex, and now the ubiquitous facsimile machine, as examples of mediated technology. There are supposedly no values when you send a fax. In other words, there is no interpretation. It is both a reproduction and a simulation. We can even pay bills by fax. The fax questions the whole nature of what was formerly *reality.* For example, what does it mean to write a letter today? In one sense I no longer write a letter. I draft it in longhand, it is then put on a disk in a computer, it is corrected, a final copy is made, I sign it, and then I put the original in a file; because I transmit the original by fax I do not waste time sending it in the post. Now if I want to pay a bill, I write a check—often to foreign countries—and I send it by fax to a bank, and it is taken care of very quickly. This means that the former conditions of reality for a written communication—signing one's name, putting the missive in an envelope, sending it as a kind of symbol of one's condition of being "in reality"—no longer exist. Receiving an original letter with the signature is no longer a necessity, nor can it any longer hold the same value. Admittedly, it has a value, but not the same value that it had before. I am told autograph seekers are more and more after that precious and rare commodity, an original signature. But because of media, the matter of originality has been called into question. Not in the way that Walter Benjamin questioned it in his ideas about originality in the age of mechanical reproduction, when he said that, in fact, a reproducible object was just as original as a handcrafted object. What Benjamin was talking about was the different aura of the reproduced object as opposed to the aura of the original, handmade object. This changed aura of the reproduction represents a paradigm shift from the mechanical era to the electronic one. It is this issue of aura, and therefore the aura of the present, that is important.

The question of the aura of a reproduction had important consequences in the arts, especially in such arts as photography. The nature of what constituted an original work of art has always been at issue: whether a serial reproduction that was signed was an original, or whether a piece of sculpture not even fabricated by the sculptor could be signed as an original. Questions have arisen about the work of architecture, ever since the fifteenth century, as regards the architect signing the drawings but not necessarily fabricating the work itself. The whole question of reproduction was rethought in the 1920s. But mechanical reproduction is not the same as mediated or electronic reproduction. One is contained in the essence of reproduction; the other has no essence at all. Mechanical reproduction still has intact a classical value system and a question of interpretation. Mediated reproduction, or simulation, has a different value system, and therefore, what we consider to be the value of that original in the mediated world is thereby thrown into question.

Sporting events are a good example of how media affect reality. I went to see one of the last baseball games in the old Comiskey Park stadium in Chicago. I went not for reason of nostalgia but rather for reasons of the *aura* of the reality. I had very good seats behind the first-base line. There is a huge television screen in center field. The screen, which used to show instant replay (and we are all instant replay junkies), now televises the entire game live. What I found myself doing was drifting off from the actual game and watching the TV because it was bigger and better. And since I was already there, who cared if I saw it on the TV? I thought I could resist watching the mediated reality, but it is much easier to watch the TV all the time than to switch back and forth to reality. Because the between-inning commercials are so good, now people do not leave the game between the innings, when the commercials are on; rather they go for their hot dogs when the game is on.

On the same weekend, I went to a football game at Soldiers Field in Chicago, again trying to see a real football stadium with real grass. What I found so amazing at that game was not that a lot of people had binoculars, but that these people were not scanning the game with their binoculars. They were not looking at the field. They were looking at the sky boxes behind us. Up there were TV sets for instant replay. And these people, with binoculars after each play, would turn around and watch the instant replay on the sky box televisions. In these circumstances you begin to ask what the reality is for these people. What do they feel about being there? What is the aura of the original? What is the sense of aura any more?

Baseball stadia once had the quality of an original. They had a sense of place. The game used to be place-sensitive. Now new ball parks are designed on a computer and there is no longer any sense of place. The dimensions are absolutely the same there are no quirks in a particular ball park. There is absolutely nothing that dictates you would need more left-handed hitters, or more right-handed hitters; everything has become homogenized. It is just the same to play in Three Rivers Stadium as it is to play in River Front Stadium or Comiskey Park, because with computerized design the place does not matter any more.

This is the real issue for all of us who deal with the environment: the traditional notions of place, space, and objects. Because media have diminished our sense of definite reality, we in turn fall victim to the manipulation. When one thinks of Disney World, one has to ask what it is. Disney World and its kin are basically media inventions. They are sold by advertising, and they are things that kids prefer, just like McDonald's hamburgers—McDonald's is another of these media franchises. In other words, my kids eat McDonald's because they are eating commercials. They do not care about the quality of the meat. It does not matter what the hamburgers taste like. They go to McDonald's to eat the commercials because their friends are all eating commercials. When Wendy's has better commercials, you may notice that the kids prefer to go to Wendy's, but it has nothing to do with the meat being better. They do not care about the quality of the food; what they are influenced by is the quality of the advertising. In other words, the media. Moreover, when you go to McDonald's you actually feel good. There is the aura of feeling good because you are with these people from the advertisements, actually eating the advertising! When you visit Disney World there is the same sense of feeling good because you are consuming the advertising about Disney World, and this therefore becomes the *real* experience. What has happened is that the people who go to theme parks have become deadened to the fact that this is not a real experience; in one sense it is very real, and it is this new reasoning one is addressing here. The media environment has become so real that the people who go to Disney World are unaware that it is, in fact, a simulated, media environment. This is because they go from media environment to media environment. They shop in a simulation of a shopping center. In the suburbs they live in a simulation of a country house. Everything that they live in is simulated.

Their worlds are already totally mediated worlds that are without value on interpretation. And if you took these people and put them in front of a real meal, let us say some real *pasta* in Italy, they would not want it, because they would not know how to deal with it; they would not have the taste or sensitivity or the condition of aureate necessity to understand what this means. Now that Disney World is being built in Paris, people will be able to take package tours of Disney World from Orlando to Paris to Tokyo without ever experiencing the *real* country.

Now is this situation a good thing or is it a bad thing? It is not really a question of value judgment—the situation simply exists all around us. We drink coffee in plastic cups; and we do not give that a second thought. We eat meals on airplanes that include milk substitute, butter substitute, maple syrup substitute, etc. When we look around us today, almost everything we eat is a substitute for something or other. I eat Ultra Slim Fast in the morning as a breakfast substitute. What we are actually experiencing is an incredible seepage into the conditions that used to make for our reality.

We need to realize what this means and, in particular, what it means for us as architects, planners, and environmentalists. The alternative, to turn the clock back and return to nostalgia, is a genuine alternative. There are a lot of us neoromantics and eccentric classicists around, who believe that we should build from a classical inventory. Some of my friends are Neoclassicist and when I go into their houses, I find they are made of the most interesting *faux* materials. One says:

"Wow, that incredible wood," only to find out that is merely *faux* stain. Is that wrong? If it looks okay, who cares if it is not real? If it does not feel like real wood, and I can actually see the pieces of plastic laminated together, what is wrong with that? Why shouldn't it be this way? In a mediated environment the question is not one of right or wrong. Media do not deal in right or wrong, but in the bottom line of what people want in the marketplace.

Arriving recently at Houston Intercontinental Airport, for this symposium, I witnessed the most amazing occurrence. On the airplane there was one solitary prisoner of war returning from Iraq. The plane was crowded with people with camera equipment, and when we landed these people were allowed to disembark first, while the P.O.W. was held back. He had to wait, so that the event of his coming home could be properly staged for the media. He was disoriented, exhausted, and upset. The media people got out, set up their cameras as if they had been on the runway all along, and began saying into their pretaping microphones, "Well, the plane has just landed," or "We are about three minutes to touchdown," and "Looks like it will be another couple of minutes before he gets out." It was quite fantastic. This whole group of people had come on the airplane from New York to stage a press conference in Houston. And the event was then taped for their sound bites in the evening. In other words, it was not even a real event; it was mediated. The media would not allow it to be real, even though it had to be staged in Houston to give it an aura of realism.

How does this affect architecture? I have a new client in Japan. We went to Japan and I asked what the program was for the building. The client mumbled something, and when I asked what he had said, I was told: "Cover." "Cover?" I repeated. "What do you mean by cover?" Shelter? That was too obvious. When I repeated my question, my client's answer was: "Magazine cover." What he wanted was to have his building appear on a magazine cover. Then it would work. I'm afraid we are, right now, designing a cover for a certain American magazine. People in architects' offices are no longer designing whole environments but, in fact, are thinking about the initial image, the cover shot, the picture postcard image, the mediated sound bite of architecture. Precisely because sound bites have taken over architecture, we no longer write a text of more than a thousand words. Get us the right photograph; plans and sections are out. It is as if you need instant replay to look at plans and sections. Clients do not want to see them. They want to see media images. Much of what I do now in my work has been taken over by the client's need to be part of a mediated environment.

Mediated environments also raise the question of a new kind time, "the time of experience." Traditionally, architecture was place-bound because people had enough time to experience the architecture. There was a condition of experience. When you go into a gallery of modern art on a Sunday afternoon anywhere in the world, whether it be the Prado in Madrid or the Metropolitan Museum in

New York, there are literally hordes of people who are passing through, in front of art, hardly stopping to look, maybe just photographing their "experiences." Most of the people are going to look at the paintings only as slides, or they are going to buy postcards of the paintings, but they will not see the art in their real experience of the building. There is no longer time for experience because people cannot concentrate long enough to have such a condition. In other words, there is no longer the possibility of viewing painting and sculpture in any kind of serious way. The same condition goes for architecture. I sat in front of the church of Sant' Andrea in Mantua about two weeks ago and watched busloads of tourists pour out with cameras, stand in front of the facade, click their cameras, then get back into the buses and drive off. They would probably never see Mantua again. What is surprising is that they even got to this little town and thought to take a picture of the facade. This is what architecture was to them, however: merely a facade. Inside, Sant' Andrea is a magnificent space. But this was not an issue, to these tourists.

Architecture is becoming time-bound in a very similar way to the sound bites of the media—time-bound in the sense that we are dealing with architecture "as event." The best architectural events that I know, the places where people are happiest, are rock concerts. People often go to rock concerts not to listen to the music, because you cannot hear the music, but just to be in that environment. A totally a new kind of environment is being projected, the environment of the event. And this environment can make people very happy, or suicidal. It turns on and off like a TV set. It never lasts very long because we no longer have the necessary attention span. The environment of the event is very much like arriving in the United Airlines Terminal at O'Hare Airport in Chicago. It has nothing to do with statistics, with this procrustean space we inhabit. It is light, it is sound, it is movement. It is simply an event.

Mediation and Return: Ambiguous Identity of the City's Edge

Paul Christensen

Here we are in Robert Venturi's modern city, not just Las Vegas but any modern city, a mediascape of office buildings and stores transformed by their corporate identities into the new language of consciousness: the sign molded in glass and light, splashed over with the insignia or characters of logos. The streets of downtown or in the commercial cores of a city are a new grammar of symbols and aggressive statements in which the materialism of things has been elevated into an architecture of job messages. Buildings are no longer mass and weight, stone and iron, but an array of sentences spelling out the consciousness of a city, what a city *means* when we enter it and use its services, consume its goods. The city is consciousness itself, that perpetual wakefulness that reaches toward the purest possible rationality in which to claim mastery over sleep, dreams, the irrational, the ambiguity of nature. The city's language of buildings and streets, of glass and light, is a declaration of ideals, the chief of which is the intellectualization of life itself, the absorption of the nonhuman into thought, which the city achieves by transforming things into words, objects into signs, the dark of nature into neon abstraction and codes.

There is no escape from the sign, the object turned into language, the thing transformed from primal materiality to a thing signified partly by its function and maker. The panorama of colors, textures, volumes making up the skyline as seen from the highway, the commuter line, the office window is one continuous matrix of consumable goods and producer logos. Where there is some stubborn holdout not symbolized into a corporate or public function—such as the lone private house with porch and peeling bay window, a television antenna tilting crazily from the roof—it stands as a reminder that the urban landscape is mortal, haunted by its own ghosts. Its own mysterious identity is something we must also try here to determine, but later on.

Enter into the mediascape and you are transformed at once—your clothing, footwear, briefcase, tote bag, all bear the logos of their producers, as you pass among the signs, painted windows, emblazoned waste bins, sponsored bus-stop benches.

You are the extension of the mediascape and continue its obsessive dynamic to disseminate consumability in a universe of transformed objects. In your own choice of symbolic apparel you advertise your class, your profession, your social attitudes, the expression of personal identity composed of already mediated objects. You are the consummation of mediated reality as the consumer in the social dynamic. Consider the man or woman *shopping*—in the act of acquiring more consumable objects but outfitted already in an array of similar ones. The shopping bags are printed with the retailers' names, the objects within brim with their logos, and the surrounding mediascape repeats the logomania of production and consumption as the shopper hurries out of the forest of signs to a residence, a neighborhood, a peripheral and moderated scale of logophilia.

Once inside the house or apartment, of course, the TV goes on, the radio may have been left on, magazines are strewn across the cocktail table or dressing room, a few gallery-exhibition prints are in frames on the wall, and the kitchen is loaded with shiny appliances—all either bearing the producer's logo or making sales pitches vigorously, incessantly, attractively. The living space is a microcosm of object-signs, the things one notices and interprets as signifiers of "self," of the user's personality. The other things—bedframe, wing chair, carpet—are the dark reminders of a primal objectivity whose disappearance into Noumea awaits.

The object bearing its maker's insignia has already passed into a new realm of the object, in which it is more subjective and abstract than those things simply made of materials and serving anonymously in their functions. The latter are untransubstantiated objects, and to value them one must study their craftsmanship and materials, their finish as things, before evaluating what they "mean" in the life of their user. But the logogenetic object takes you partly away from the materiality of the thing into its noumenal career as a sign. To the degree that Mr. Coffee signifies an automatic coffeemaker of a certain kind, as opposed to a Braun Aromaster, each imparting different qualitative and stylistic nuances—that is, psychological subtleties, to the user—that is the margin by which the object has disappeared, been transvaluated into ambience, psychic space. As the mediascape devours the literal materiality around it, it transforms the somber house or brick factory into human consciousness—as air, glass gleaming chrome and plastic, materials that drive things into the sign world of mediation.

Light is the metaphor of transformation of objects into signs. The city is light disseminated throughout its commercial core, fading to the edges where primal objectivity stands mutely under the baleful glimmers of streetlights and porch lamps. Neon light is the archetype of spiritual transformation of goods, consumable objects; even the "lite" foods and beverages sold as dietary aids reinforce this image of light, the lightness of being.

The city resides in nature as a clearing of light, a center of radiance replacing what was once spiritual light. It has become a neon cathedral amidst the dark borders surrounding it. Bathed in floodlighting, the city lifts itself out of darkness as a symbol of purified human consciousness against a backdrop of obdurate earthliness and ambiguity. The land under a farm or a dwelling is less transferable, more slowly obtained, and thus darker, more substantial than the array of commodities on their blazing altars at discount shops, in mall windows, on display at airport terminals—commodities whose fixity in the order of things is as fragile as ideas, ephemeral perceptions.

Objects in the city, including the physical structure of the city—streets, buildings, highways—are all rising toward the realm of speech; some have already turned into speech. What is a billboard of itself? It is only the backing of a momentary statement that is always changing its assertion to the public streaming below it. The lone pillar that blazes its neon message, EATS, out of the dark shoulders of a freeway is no more than a suggestion bursting out of the dark of the body. The city is thus a realm of consciousness, a place of language grounded in a vocabulary of desired goods and services.

At the center of commerce, everything is made into altars and chapels bathed in spiritual light offering transubstantiations of nature. The modern city is the essential expression of the humanist paradigm: man as god, whose powers over the simple fact of life are absolute. The city concentrates human expressions of nature, human possession of the objective world. The selling of the objects it transforms is affirmation of human divinity, a declaration that things are elevated in value by human manipulation. Objects are blessed by imagination and the refinements of manufacture; they have been humanized and placed within a finite system of circulation among those who can afford them. Where the city dims out into poverty, violence, addiction, ignorance, degradation, the sacred precincts fade away and the natural world resumes. That way leads to darkness, the opposite pole of radiant human transcendence.

The city encloses its own negation by embracing vacant lots, shacks, tenements, abandoned buildings, the gaunt shells of burned-out neighborhoods destroyed by riots and urban decay. Radiance becomes opacity here; trash fills the streets and open spaces, where once expressive objects return to matter again as compost and rusting metal. At the the other end of the department store's altars of radiant goods stands the thrift shop with its mounds of dark, tangled clothing, broken clocks and battered toys, books with their covers torn off. The suits donated by the local Sears store have had their labels ripped out; other goods have lost their identity along the way. The passage to oblivion begins with anonymity, uniformity. The mounded coats and sweaters under the trembling violet dimness of a fluorescent tube are of one substance and color—generic clothing useful in covering the limbs of human beings, no more. Their claim to a function is vague and undifferentiated, like the human beings who wear them. They form one part of the category of coverings—including rags, animal skins, fiber, and hair.

Out on the perimeters of Detroit, in a black neighborhood that has been the locale of perpetual house fires and the slower grind of devastation brought on by crack, stand a cluster of houses decorated by the artist Tyree Guyton. You do not understand Guyton's intentions until you thread your way through the dingy neighborhoods that surround his work. If you look carefully you will note that the burned-out hulks still possess some evidence of human occupation: the doll left dangling from a shrub's withered branch, the upturned and wheelless body of a wagon, the tangle of coathangers someone pitched from a window as the house blazed away in the night. These and myriad other details have been concentrated into Guyton's houses, where all the detritus of anonymity and oblivion have been piled up in vast dunes of junk. The houses, in some places sloshed with garish paint, are still visible as traditional American houses. They possess their old domestic personalities under the heaps of trash, junk, broken toys; they stand there as gaunt skeletons onto which have been nailed everything that drifts out of sanctity and ends as death. The house has become the repository of things returning to nature. Guyton perceived the flow of energies in the American city, the reverse course of ideas as they part gradually from the light and language at the metropolitan center and decay out of consciousness into memory, and then to forgetfulness and opaque death.

Guyton, like the Chicano artist Simon Rodilla, discovered the limit of the city and erected a monument of its own evidence to point it out. The rain pours down on the vast accumulation of detritus, breaking it down slowly into earth again. But already one detects that in this stripped language the objects return to something like their original ambiguity once more, as they do in Rodilla's Watts towers, where we see bits of tile, wire, glass fragments broken down further and made into steeplelike projections. Both Guyton and Rodilla are the artist as scavenger, gleaners of decayed consciousness the moment it returns to the realm of earth and death. Guyton's doll faces, limbs, and torsos, the scattered parts of rejected toys, the rusting wash tubs and battered mattresses, the broken instruments, tools, gadgets, are objects that have lost their function as consciousness; they are once more part of the potentiality of nature as they fade back into ground. In their anonymous masses they return to a primal state where decay has obliterated consciousness and left only the unconscious mystique of the "thing" itself, the archetype within its melted and distorted flesh.

This is the unmediated reality of decay and death, where awareness ceases to be driven by the ego and devolves instead into memory and images, the ghosts of things. At this end of the city things wear their flesh loosely and attend more to what is myth and archetype than to what is life. Even the new goods that are for sale are indifferent materializations of objects—generic objects like can openers, bottle stoppers, bicycles, the brand names of which are meaningless. These things come from cultures in which religions diffuse the ego, from Buddhist Asia and Mayan-Catholic Mexico, and are uniform in their shoddiness and vagueness. They are used and disposed of quickly, as they pass from momentary existence back into the earth again. The peripheral subcity devours the consciousness at the center, sucking down the light and disposing of it as junk, offal, pollution, clutter, house fires.

The city generates consciousness and devours it at its other limit; it produces the human world and digests it in its lower body among the ghettoes and back streets, and out across its hinterlands. Consciousness literalizes nature and transforms it into the light and language of the ego; decay brings objects back to their material opaqueness, in which the spirit of nature reenters and object as the force of ambiguity and creativity, even as it decomposes. The sight of rotting artifacts in a field, or behind the squalid shacks of an urban wasteland, is a vision of another will imposing itself, reclaiming human awareness.

Generality reigns in this twilight of the mediascape; nothing is particularized, everything is multifoliate and illogical, a realm of dreams, illusions, hallucinations, altered mental states. The ground is unconscious, archetypal beneath the run-down neighborhoods. It is where one finds the grotesque body; the obese and deformed live here. Death is exposed; the dogs and cats decompose quietly in the weeds. The graveyard is haunted with spectres; the trestles stir at night with the homeless, the tramps, prostitutes, the mentally ill. The individual no longer exit at these wilderness limits of the city; he or she is swallowed up in work forces, in the armed services, or in gangs.

At either end of the city, the object fades out of reality when pushed too far. It rises into the evanescent glare of consciousness at the center, and decomposes into darkness and archetypal mystery at the edge. What is jewelled and glittering in the windows of downtown stores becomes rough, slapdash, generalized in the mean streets. Either way, a thing tends toward extinction: toward the literalness of the ego, or plummeting to the bottom of the body to become earth, fertile, decaying soil. The polarity is absolute, a dialectic of human awareness that defies architectural novelty and social alternatives to its system of relations. To build in the city is to participate in one or the other of its dynamics—to drive life upward into ideas, or down toward the irrationality of earth.

If there is a middle state within the dialectic of urban life, where the new is possible, it lies somewhere in the process by which things begin their fate toward either end. The making of a building is the inevitable act of raising or lowering materiality to its fate—but where Peter Eisenman has possibly hit upon a third term of the city is by deconstructing the act of making itself. The buildings he designs are trembling, vibrating, coming apart as if forcibly held back from completing their goal as ideational expressions. The shape is disturbed as if a force had been designed into the construction that aimed at holding it down, forcing its fate backward toward earth even as it surges toward the center and light. This creates a building whose sentence stammers and partially deconstructs itself—as the only means for asserting its existence against the fate of rationalization and disappearance.

Eisenman's buildings are deliberately vague and contradictory expressions; they ignore architectural clarity (predictability) as the only means of escaping ideation, spiritual oblivion. The crooked portico, the fractured facia, the wobbling hallways and deformed staircases are forms of the irrational built into thought, language; they are the elements of the dream that pull consciousness back to earth. Eisenman's structural poetics introduce surreal imagery into the urban structure, and thus bring the human house away from light and part of the way back to Tyree Guyton's houses, where the surreal and the dream state have triumphed wholly over human intellect. Eisenman will hold the house back from that fate as well; his house is pulled apart by the twin will of the city, by the ego and the soul.

Lost Utopia: Thoughts on the Dilemma of the Modern City

Kaisa Broner-Bauer

> An object or an act becomes real only insofar as it imitates or repeats an archetype. Thus, reality is acquired solely through repetition or participation; everything which lacks an exemplary model is "meaningless."
>
> — Mircea Eliade, 1949

In the first part of the nineteenth century, it was Victor Hugo who, from a literary point of view, revived discussion about architecture as a symbolic language and its destiny in the modern world. Hugo was a contemporary of Hegel, who in the 1820s was teaching philosophy in Berlin. Their respective views were in fact quite similar. Both of them also prophetically foresaw the death of art. While Hegel alluded to the spiritual impoverishment of modern times, for Hugo it was expressly the advancement of printing techniques that was to dethrone architecture—the major art which during the first six thousand years of human history had recorded all its great ideas. *Ceci tuera cela,* this will kill that, the book will kill the edifice, was Hugo's cruel prophecy.

The Birth of the Modern Concept of the City and City Planning

> When man understands the art of seeing, he can trace the spirit of an age and the features of a king in the knocker on a door.
>
> —Victor Hugo, 1831

In his novel *The Hunchback of Notre Dame* (1831) Hugo gives a masterly description of Paris at the height of the Gothic period, and in doing so he traces not only the spirit of the Middle Ages but also the spirit of that city, a "chronicle in stone." In medieval society, as Hugo states, all the existing material, intellectual, and spiritual forces of humanity focused on the same thing: architecture, the physical existential environment of man. "He who was born a poet became an architect," was Hugo's conclusion crystallizing the spirit of those times.

Let us not forget that the Paris in which Victor Hugo lived when writing his famous novel was still an integrated historic city that had not yet lost its medieval look—although Hugo severely criticized its general physiognomy, which in his eyes was "a collection of parts from several different ages, the finest of all having disappeared." But there was an even greater threat to it, and that must have been felt by Hugo, talented as he was in the "art of seeing." Paris, like London, was the capital of a country in a strong industrialization process, and as such was to become subjected to enormous change. It happened, indeed, only two decades after the publication of *The Hunchback of Notre Dame,* and Hugo, for political reasons, had then to leave his city and go into exile. During the next twenty years, under Napoleon III, Paris was totally transformed, and became the model city for modernization in the western world.

There are three or four factors reflecting the atmosphere of Paris in the nineteenth century—and they much resemble those pertaining in other big European cities of that epoch confronted with industrial development. The first three factors are: historicism or the eclectic use of revival styles; constructivism or the development of modern building technology; and the birth of modern building typology, as a function of new social development. The fourth factor, which especially interests us here, concerns urban development. It was in the nineteenth century that the phenomenon of a truly big city came into existence. As the concept of the modern metropolis was born, the first steps taken to resolve its problems signified for their part the starting point of modern city planning and design.

One thing must be made clear: if the roots of modern architecture may be sought in the radical Neoclassicism of the end of the eighteenth century, in the "architecture of liberty," and in the functionalist ideology of the nineteenth century—that is, in the times of nascent industrialism—this was not the case for modern city planning and design. Modern city planning was not born at the same time as industrial society. One may assert to the contrary that it developed afterwards. In other words, modern city planning in its early stages was typified by the fact that it proposed improvements only at the moment when, as a consequence of a massive transformation process, industrializing urban societies had been driven into an intolerable and virtually insoluble state of crisis.

The origins of modern city planning are in fact twofold: technical and moral. In that sense, two kinds of factors influenced the contents of the first plans made to improve the prevailing conditions: there were, on the one hand, factors linked with the difficulties and imbalances inherent in trying to control urbal development, and on the other hand, those linked with a growing rejection of the inadequacies of the existing situation and a desire to take active steps to ameliorate things. In Europe, such conditions were especially prevalent in England as well as France, because in those two countries the industrialization process took place earlier than elsewhere.

Utopian Models versus Paternalistic Planning
The first attempts to repair the unsatisfactory conditions of the industrial city

represent these two opposing lines. In the first place, an important role was played by the so-called Utopians who took up arms directly against what they considered the cause of the problems, determined to build an ideal society—a society that would eliminate poverty, epidemics, and unhygienic living conditions. To this group belonged such men as Robert Owen, Saint-Simon, Charles Fourier, Etienne Cabet, and Jean-Baptiste Godin. Pioneers of a social way of thinking, they provide us with the first models of humanitarian environmental planning.

Robert Owen (1771–1858), an Englishman, was the first and perhaps the most significant Utopian. He was a self-made man who achieved success as an industrialist and had an important political career. He had a passion for improving factory workers' living conditions and made various innovations with that end in view. After 1810 Owen planned a model for an ideal community—an independent, self-supporting village in the countryside, with its own factories and social services for 800–1200 inhabitants. The architectural layout of the village comprised a central square surrounded by low residential buildings on each side. Dwellings were planned in detail, right down to heating and ventilation. There were communal kitchens and restaurants, a hospital and a church, schools, and other public services located along the middle axis of the complex. Owen's village was an idealized vision for a better future. It was the first modern attempt at a coherent community plan, integrating social and economic aspects, as well as architecture.

The Frenchman Charles Fourier (1772–1837) for his part conceived a seven-phase utopian system tending toward universal harmony. The sixth phase of the process comprised the building of an ideal city. Although Fourier did not possess the financial means to realize any of his idealistic visions, he did make detailed plans for a model city, based on the principle of zoning. Fourier's city had a circular plan divided into three different zones: commercial and administrative functions in the center, industrial activities in the surrounding belt, and housing areas in the suburbs. Each zone was separated from the preceding one by a green belt. Building density was defined according to the nature of the zone. All the buildings were freestanding collective structures. Facades were uniform, the disposition of the whole, including concentrated social services, being conceived in terms of Fourier's socialistic ideals, based on a collectivist approach to life. His model was to exert enormous influence on the concept of the modern city. He may be considered as the initial exponent of the principle of space division determined by functional differentiation.

Fourier also published plans for an ideal community, a collectivist village that he called a *phalanstére*. The village was conceived for about 1500–1600 inhabitants living in accommodation similar to that of a hotel, organized on the basis of collective services. Architecturally it looked like a royal palace, with a symmetrical plan around a square. Its most interesting detail was a gallery street, an idea that

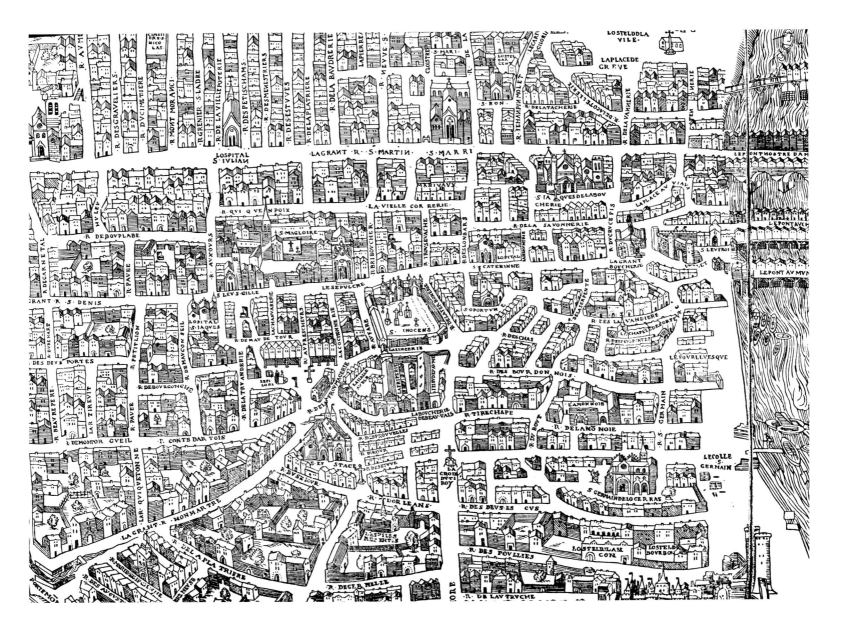

Fig. 3.1. Medieval Paris at the entrance of the New Age. Plan by Olivier Truschet and Germane Hoyau, 1552.

has been much made use of during this century by modern architects, notably Le Corbusier.

There were several *phalanstéres* built in France and abroad, but none of them survived for long. Jean Baptiste Godin (1817–89), a compatriot of Fourier, was more successful in carrying out these ideas. He adopted Fourier's initial model, transformed it, and called it a *familistère*. Godin's ideal was tailored to a simpler and more individualistic way of life. Every family had its own dwelling, but was

18

provided with collective services, including a common kitchen and restaurant, a kindergarten, schools, and a theater. Godin mixed different uses within the same area, avoiding Fourier's rigid pattern of functionally distinct zones. A *familistère* was built in Guise for about 400 families in the 1880s. It was a very important experiment, without doubt the most successful realization of nineteenth-century socialistic ideas.

There were many other attempts to describe or to create an ideal city or society in the second half of the last century. It was a popular theme favored by authors and social thinkers of the epoch. Despite their high-minded social intentions and leftist ideology, the Utopians began to be criticized even by socialist partisans. They also finally fell into disfavor with the working class, mainly because of the influence of Marx and Engels who condemned the Utopians' experiments as "reformatory" rather than revolutionary. This view was notably adopted by Engels in his essay on the "housing question" (*Wohnungsfrage*) published in 1872. In accordance with Marxian premises Engels stated that the problems of workers' bad housing conditions could not be resolved without a total socialistic revolution.

Another attitude toward the problems of the big industrial city—an opposite tendency to that of the Utopians—was that taken by city officials who in the second half of the nineteenth century resorted to different measures in order to try to control urban development, which was becoming a more and more serious problem. The first legislation aimed at improving unhygienic housing conditions of working-class areas were created at the time. The Public Health Act of 1878 in England offers an example of this. The idea was to use the force of law to define the norms for controlling the right to build, density, building height, and the like. But the effect of this legislation was rather depressing—the formation of monotonous housing areas, the beginning of a certain kind of urban development process, the final results of which are all too familiar to us today.

In France, the revolution of 1848 provided a crucial phase. After this turning point, city planning became a one-sided technical function controlled by the ruling social class. It was a pity that Marxian criticism condemned the Utopians. By doing so, the Marxists cut off the unique living connection between politics and environmental and social planning that was characteristic of the Utopians' experiments. Instead, a paternalistic line of city planning became dominant, manifesting itself especially in the politics of big public projects, such as the urban renewal program realized by Baron Haussmann under Napoleon III.

The Formation of the Modern City
> So also the historical meaning of its architecture is daily wearing away. . . .
> Art becomes nothing but skin clothing bones. It dies miserably.
> —Victor Hugo, 1831

One may discern five phases in the formation of the modern city in Europe, from the mid-nineteenth century to the first decades of the twentieth, and these phases coincide with the evolution of the concepts of modern city planning and design. They culminated in the following developments:

Transformation of Paris under Napoleon III (1853–82)
Paris was the first city that was "regularized" according to the demands of the industrial age. The key words of the urban renewal program carried out by Baron Haussmann were strategy, hygiene, and traffic, as well as the expansion of the city toward the west. The traditional medieval urban structure had to give way to a new vision according to which the old Parisian blocks were mercilessly torn down along straight lines drawn upon the city map. Haussmann however did not completely reject the urban tradition of the Baroque. The closed type of block was retained although its form now was usually triangular. This "Haussmannian" block form resulted from the plan of radial streets which traversed the densely built urban fabric, connecting the strategic points of the city one to another. The new airy streets bordered by bougeois types of apartment buildings became the arteries of the rising middle-class Paris. The working class were forced to retreat to the periphery. This was the starting point of social division of space—the beginning of "social zoning" in Paris.

Garden City Sections of London
When Ebenezer Howard published his book *Garden Cities of Tomorrow* in 1898, it very soon became the "bible" of a new ideal—the picturesque, human-scale city settled in the midst of a natural landscape, with trees and greenery. Although Howard's model for a garden city was an independent unit and not a suburb or a simple neighborhood, the first "garden cities" built following his ideas at the beginning of this century were just London suburban areas. They were planned by Raymond Unwin, who adapted Howard's garden city ideal to the concrete situation of the growing metropolis at that time. In the new garden city sections of London, the traditional, hierarchic organization of space was maintained, while in detailing the ideas of the Austrian Camillo Sitte were followed to produce picturesque effects. An interesting new invention was a "half-open" block structure with low houses grouped around a half-public courtyard or a blind alley. The English garden city ideology along with Sitte's detailing notions was to have a strong influence later on, notably on the development of the German *Siedlungen.*

Expansion of Amsterdam (1913–34)
In the years between 1850 and 1920 the number of Amsterdam's inhabitants increased threefold, from 230,000 to 690,000. In 1913 plans for the city's expansion were prepared, with H. P. Berlage as its leading architect. What Berlage proposed was in fact a synthesis of two plans, one dealing with the monumental organization of the whole, and the other with picturesque detailing. While one may still discern, to a certain degree, the influence of Sitte and the English garden city ideal on Berlage's proposal, the type of block he chose was far more "closed" and

in that sense more "urban" than the half-open blocks chosen by Unwin for his London plans. Berlage's architecture also clearly had a more urban character: the buildings were designed in a spatial continuum connected with the densely built existing urban fabric of Amsterdam. Berlage's solution was quite wise. Without rejecting the traditional concept of the European city, he succeeded in creating a synthesis of the traditional and the modern—a valid vision for the future development of Amsterdam.

German Siedlungen

The first *Siedlungen* were built in Frankfurt am Main in the years 1925–30. At that time the city's leading planner was Ernst May. In the mid-1920s he started to prepare new types of plans for housing areas, which radically broke away from the city's traditional morphology and spatial order. While May in his first *Siedlungen,* such as Römerstadt, still continued the garden city tradition as laid down by Ebenezer Howard, Raymond Unwin, and Camillo Sitte, he soon thereafter adopted a more rational grid plan. In his later *Siedlungen* May placed modern cubic buildings in the middle of wholly open quadrangular blocks, completely disregarding Frankfurt's traditional densely built urban form.

May's *Siedlungen* were planned according to the principles of CIAM, as defined at the Congrès International de l'Architecture Moderne (the Frankfurt congress) of 1927. These principles were to have a long-lasting effect on the image of Frankfurt as well as other German cities, and not only those which were destroyed in World War II and rebuilt during the following decades. As suggested by Manfredo Tafuri, May's work may be interpreted as the ultimate expression of

Fig. 3.2. Ernst May's *Siedlung* Westhausen, Frankfurt am Main, 1929–31 (Frankfurt City Archives).

21

concrete politicization of architecture. In fact May was well known for his social-ist opinions, and Nazi propaganda also did not fail to condemn the Frankfurt *Siedlungen* as constructed Socialism. This was to encourage a simplistic "black and white" ideology to prevail among modern architects, identifying the use of traditional urban patterns and architectural forms with political conservatism.

La Cité Radieuse
The evolution of the concept of the modern city reaches its culmination in the projects of Le Corbusier for the "Radiant City" (*cité radieuse*). In his visualiza-tion of the modern city the traditional European city structure was definitely abandoned. What Le Corbusier proposed was a scheme of urban highways and tower buildings scattered in a park—in other words, the suburbanization of the city.

Although Le Corbusier's vision of the modern city developed gradually, his ear-lier designs, such as "A Contemporary City" (*Une Ville Contemporaine*, 1922) and "Plan for a City of Three Million Inhabitants" (1922) were already extremely radical. In a similar way, his proposal for the historical neighborhood of Marais in Paris, the famous *Plan Voisin* of 1925, was a provocative demonstration of in-difference toward—and at the same time a complete failure to understand—the values of the traditional European city and urban culture. The new kind of ur-ban structure introduced by Le Corbusier was based on the modern, open-space conception which had originally made its appearance in architecture, especially in the designs of Frank Lloyd Wright and Mies van der Rohe. In the name of technical and material progress, the traditional European concept of the city was declared outmoded, unhealthy, and obsolescent.

Lost Utopia

> Man constructs according to an archetype. Not only do his city or his tem-ple have celestial models: the same is true of the entire region that he inhab-its. . . . This participation by urban cultures in an archetypal model is what gives them their reality and their validity.
>
> —Mircea Eliade, 1949

The aim of the nineteenth-century Utopians was to construct an ideal society. In their projects there was at the same time an ideological and an idealistic connec-tion between the social content and the architectural form. The other, opposing tendency represented by conservative city officials was to try to improve the exist-ing conditions of the industrial city by eliminating its worst defects. Their aim was to avoid social revolution by adopting certain progressive ideas.

Modern city planning, like modernism in general, has been influenced by both of these tendencies. From the Utopians the modern movement adopted the idea of utopia as a driving force, but it became reduced to a utopia of form, while

the social content of the revolutionized form could be just anything. For the nineteenth-century Utopians, the cultural continuity offered by retention of the traditional forms of architectural vocabulary was not felt to be a threat. For them, architecture acquired new meaning as a synthesis of traditional forms and new social contents—as an expression of the will to create an ideal society.

For the modern movement, on the contrary, a revolution in the external forms of architecture became the principal tenet. As a result, form and meaning became estranged from each other, and form became meaningless. The effect was rapid and worldwide because architects and planners associated with the modern movement adopted its absolute paradigms of form, which were widely disseminated through the theses of CIAM, with its strong and simple slogans. Form followed functionalist ideology and modern technology. The cultural values of the city were forgotten and cast aside.

The results are well known to us. City planning today is a professional field which lays emphasis on the technical aspects of the environment through a more or less narrow interpretation of regulations tailored to bureaucratic and political purposes. Instead of any real social utopia or an ideal, there exist a myriad of rules corresponding to the requirements of market forces and the accumulation of capital. Under present conditions, city planners cannot but try to achieve a bal-

Fig. 3.4. The city empty of meaning—La Défense in Paris. Photo: Kaisa Broner-Bauer.

ance between the different parties interested in consuming urban space. When the city becomes an object of manipulation and merchandise, art can only perish miserably.

Let us return to the title of this paper, "Lost Utopia." What does *utopia* really mean? It is a Greek word describing a place which does not exist: *ou-topos*. In literature the word has also acquired other meanings: it is an imaginary place, country, or society where peace, happiness, and perfect order are prevailing characters. Thomas More was the first to use the word in the latter sense, in his famous novel *Utopia* published in 1516, which was an enigmatic, discreetly satirical account of an ideal society. In present-day language the word "utopian" may also mean an attempt to reform the world, or a project that is not based on real conditions and therefore is impossible to realize.

A typical trait of modern city planning, especially since the influence of CIAM and until very recently, has been an aspiration to realize some kind of utopian view—a vision of life in the future, a vision of the city in the times to come. Its starting point is thus utopian, in the literal sense that it is nonexistent, while not taking into account the existing circumstances of time and place, and the people for whom the plans are being made. The utopian visions have been based on different kinds of programs for future development, often totally illusory, prepared with the aid of sociology and other modern prognostic sciences, since planners no longer know the people for whom they conceive a living environment. This kind of concern for the facts of the future only, excluding the values transmitted from the past, denotes a materialistic attitude and an indifference to nonmaterial human needs.

The problem of the modern city and city planning is utopia itself—the nonexistent place, lacking the qualities of a real place. And this lack creates its own symptomatic effects. One of them is the obsession with place and time that is felt by modern humanity, reflecting the illness of our age. Contemporary people have lost contact with the place where we live, a contact of creative interaction that would reinforce our identity and give us the feeling of belonging in that place; and we have lost the metaphysical sense of time. The adoption of a utopian paradigm of form, a form without an archetypal content which therefore is empty of meaning, has led to an impasse—literally to a place that does not exist, because it does not have the spiritual qualities that would give it life.

There are of course many reasons for the development of the present-day situation—historical, philosophical, and religious reasons which go beyond the ideas, aspirations, or failures of modernism alone. It is a long process beginning at the Renaissance, a process of secularization and desacralization, when people started to lose contact with the sacred dimension of life. Before that, everything that had meaning was sacred, including not only art but labor as well. Art was creation, and creation meant repetition of sacred models of archetypes, which were transmitted by tradition and mythology from one generation to another. By abandoning tradition and ancient myths, and elevating the logic of human reason in the place of God, we lost something precious. As a result, we were not able to create any more. What was left was only history and the utopian future. Since humanity was no longer able to create, the only thing to do was to fall back on reasoning in order to anticipate the facts of the future and give them shape—or to re-create by quotation.

Consider the history of architecture from the Renaissance to the present, includ-

Fig. 3.5. A Postmodern street—Saalgasse in
Frankfurt am Main. Photo: Joachim Keute.

ing the nineteenth-century revival styles and the Postmodernism of today. While the Renaissance created a new vision of antiquity, in the last analysis all these stylistic developments, except modernism, used quotation, Postmodernism finally being an art of quotation *par excellence*. Indeed, after the ideological collapse of modernism, Postmodern architects have been or still are obsessed with the goal of creating a meaningful architecture. But when one is not able to create anew, all that is left is to quote the meaningful forms of the past.

The Dilemma of the Modern City

> The face of Europe was changed. Well! The face of architecture changed too. Like civilization, it turned a page, and the new spirit of the times found her ready to write its new dictates.
>
> —Victor Hugo, 1831

We live in an age of frenetic change. Not only are habits and social and economic structures changing, but the face of our living environment and the value system on which our everyday life is based are being replaced at an accelerated pace—like industrial products. André Malraux was obviously right when he said that the twentieth century represents the high point in the development of materialism; it is a dark age in which the spiritual values are disappearing. Malraux predicted that the twenty-first century would be an age of spiritual growth. Let us hope.

If city planning is to become an art again, and the city a work of art, first we must rediscover a spiritual basis for our life. This is the challenge of our age. Contemporary humankind has no ideal; we do not believe in utopia—an idealized place—any more, nor do we believe in God. But we suffer a feeling of loss, and are obsessed by finding a meaning for what we do. We feel a need to participate in something valuable, to belong in a place and to sense time, in order to find a significance for our lives.

Lost utopia is the dilemma of the modern city. There is no ideal for the future but, nevertheless, the future must be planned here and now. Instead of a utopian vision based on factual calculation, the present situation should now be the starting point.

There is no choice: first, we must stop destroying our cultural heritage and work on preserving the values of place where they still exist. Second, we need to reconstruct a real philosophy of the city, in relation to the archetypes of the "eternal present." We have to accept the movement of time, with its stratifications in the past, the present, and the future. Perhaps then the paternalistic line of planning which has left its marks on the modern city will finally die of its own spiritual emptiness. Then we may start believing in utopia again: a utopia that is not simply utopian in image, but a real ideal for the spiritual well-being of people and society.

References

Benevolo, Leonardo, *Aux sources de l'urbanisme moderne,* André and Frances Descamps, trs., (Horizon de France, 1972).

Castex, J., J. Ch. Depaule, and Ph. Panerai, *Formes urbaines: de l'îlot á la barre* (Paris: Dunod, 1977).

Eliade, Mircea, *The Myth of the Eternal Return or Cosmos and History,* by Willard R. Trask, tr., (Arkana/Penguin Books, 1989).

Howard, Ebenezer, *Garden Cities of ToMorrow* (1902; F. J. Osborn, ed., Cambridge, Mass.: MIT Press, 1965).

Hugo, Victor, *The Hunchback of Notre Dame,* (1831; Walter J. Cobb, tr., New American Library/Penguin Books).

Le Corbusier, *Urbanisme,* (Paris: Editions G. Crés et Cie, 1925).

More, Thomas, *Utopia,* ed. by George M. Logan and Robert M. Adams (Cambridge Univ. Press, 1989).

Tafuri, Manfredo, *Architecture and Utopia; Design and Capitalist Development,* (Barbara Luigia La Penta, tr., Cambridge, Mass.: MIT Press, 1976).

28
Kaisa Broner-Bauer

The Present Urban Predicament
Colin Rowe

Alberti's statement that the house is a small city and the city is a large house per-haps *should* be true; but, certainly, there scarcely seems to have been any such correspondence between the architecture and the urbanism sponsored by the modern movement. A quasiprivate world of mostly domestic architecture which often disclosed an elaborate concern for contingency and spatial involution, with a more public world which usually displayed an almost complete impatience with the empirical fabric of the city, with any existence of idiosyncrasy: such is the seeming paradox, complex house–simple city, which seems to have been pro-moted; but which, for the most part, remained unobserved. For the simple city was, of course, not so much a city as it was a psychological construction.

> I have a vision of the future, chum.
> The workers flats in fields of soya beans,
> Towering up like silver pencils, score on score,
> While surging millions hear the challenge come
> From microphones in communal canteens
> No right, no wrong, all's perfect, evermore.

To quote John Betjeman is to make more or less appropriate commentary upon the city propounded by modern architecture; and to add another question is to make still more appropriate commentary upon the present day. The second quotation is from Baudelaire: "There may be a subtle joy in deserting an old cause in order to find out what one will feel like in serving a new one."

So it might be supposed that, as of now, many persons involved with architecture and urbanism are experiencing this "subtle joy." For we are, presently, the wit-nesses of a great *dégringolade*. Modern architecture which was once to be seen as among the conspicuous hopes of humanity has suddenly come to seem, at best, incredible, and at worst, a lamentable aberration. And although this cannot mean that all notions of modernism have been flushed away—(notions of mod-ernism are too complex to be readily dismissable)—it must mean that all kinds of old certainties are vanishing and that neither action nor observation can any longer rely upon the simple faith of what it is sometimes tempting to call the heroic days. The vision of the future, the fantasy of the infallibly programmed society in which unhappiness and tragedy are forbidden, has dimmed. Modern architecture and the city which it proposed no longer elicit "a willing suspension of disbelief."[1] And so we have the Art Deco revival, the exponents of Postmodernism, of super-Mannerism, of *Architettura Razionale,* and of all the other practitioners of Baudelaire's "subtle joy." We have the threats of modern architecture's impending demise, alternatively the information of its extinction; and, though much of all this may be journalistic and graphic maneuver and much, because of its gratuitous triviality, may inspire yet another wave of revulsion, we have still acquired a little crop of possibly premature obituaries. And, though I have scarcely read them (I find Postmodernism a somewhat opaque concept), I must now attempt, as an opening strategy, to imagine one of my own. Its conclusion might read something like this:

> We may ascribe her death (modern architecture is surely a she) to the ingenuousness of her temperament. Displaying an extraordinary addiction to towers and completely unconstructed spaces, when young she possessed a high and romantically honorable idea of life and her excess of sensibility could only lead to later chagrin. Like one of Jane Austen's more extreme heroines—though she was simultaneously morally reserved, passionate, and artless—it was her juvenile notion that, once she was perfectly wedded to society, this so much desired husband would, by the influence of her example, become redeemed of errors, tractable, pliant, and ready to act with her in any philanthropy which she might have in mind. But the marriage did not prove to be a success. Modern architecture was admired by society but not for what she conceived to be her inherent virtues. Her spouse was attracted by her many external charms but was utterly unwilling to award recognition of what she conceived to be the ethical principle of her being. And, in spite of the elevated model which she offered, he remained stubbornly confirmed in his old ways. Moral regeneration he did *not* seek. For him the ethical posture of modern architecture was too much like that of a Victorian heroine and, correspondingly, he looked for his delinquent pleasures elsewhere. He, society, was in no way ready to envisage those limpid possibilities of the New Jerusalem which she still so enthusiastically advertised and, as she continued, he increasingly became fatigued. Indeed, he (society) came to discover that, though admired, he too was not accepted; and, gradually, the rift because irretrievable. Not surprising, therefore, should be modern architecture's agitated and long decline; but, though this death was to be expected, it is greatly to be regretted and the extinction of this once pristine creature (with her elaborately Victorian standards) has been desperately sad to witness. But, a late nineteenth-century character and never fully knowing it, she addressed herself to a moral condition of permanent rapture, to an ecstatic condition which could only endanger her frail physique; and, to repeat, excessive sensibility abused by inadequate experience, motivated by a

quasireligious sentiment not well understood, and complicated by the presence of physics envy, *Zeitgeist* worship, object fixation, and stradaphobia must be considered the greatest factors contributing to the demise.

Physics envy, *Zeitgeist* worship, object fixation, and stradaphobia, I believe, are none of them yet known to the clinical diagnosticians of what used to be called "the faculty." I owe the first term to Denise Scott-Brown and the second to David Watkin.[2] A number of years ago, speaking at a symposium in the Museum of Modern Art, Denise Scott-Brown proceeded to attack, quite violently, a state of mind which, with obvious derivations from Freud, she designated "physics envy": the idea that architecture could ever be elevated, or reduced, to the level of that most "certain" of sciences. David Watkin, in criticizing the Hegelian component of modern architecture's apologetic, the conception of the architect as sensitive antenna, humble pencil, obedient planchette, just simply transcribing the utterings and mutterings of "the spirit of the age," has spoken of *Zeitgeist* worship.

We will consult only "the facts" (physics envy) and we will experience no serious epistemological concern as to what the substance of these "facts" may be. Simultaneously, and without any sense of incongruity or inhibition, we will happily submit ourselves to "the will of the epoch" (*Zeitgeist* worship) without too many questions as to whether this will is substantial, singular or manifold, or indeed anything other than a highly unempirical, historical abstraction.

So physics envy and *Zeitgeist* worship which together (let us wait for direction from outside ourselves) constitute an implicit denial of free will, are almost certainly to be related to our present incapacity to innovate—(but I am *merely* the *agent* of "science" and "destiny")—to our present conception of ourselves as victims.

However this is to digress, since it is not so much with the morale of modern architecture as with the physique of its related city that this present discussion is concerned. And if Scott-Brown and Watkin have, as I believe, correctly diagnosed the most debilitating of modern architecture's psychoses, I must now attempt to give substance to my own terminology. Two images—the corner of the unbuilt Library and Administration Building at IIT which excited so much enthusiasm circa 1950, and the corner of the courtyard of the Ducal Palace at Urbino—might serve to initiate a preliminary discussion about the style of attack and the physical limitations of modern architecture.

We are here presented with both an outer angle and an inner angle, and both conditions are argued with almost obsessive clarity. However, though one may admire them both, for present purposes this parallel is equipped with a prejudice which might be quite simply stated: modern architecture and, following its lead, related urban practice has been enormously preoccupied with the outer angle, presumably aggressive and protuberant, and has scarcely been able to involve itself with the inner angle, possibly passive and receptive.

Now, no doubt, this statement could be made to bear a completely monstrous overload; but, instead of that, all that I here wish to extricate from it is that the tradition of modern architecture has tended to produce objects rather than spaces, has been highly involved with problems of the built solid and very little with problems of the unbuilt void, that the inner angle which cradles space has scarcely been among its concerns. Which further statement may introduce the pressing question: just how to make a city if all buildings proclaim themselves as objects, and how many object-buildings can be aggregated before comprehension fails?

Ingenuity versus Contingency
Although the principal victim of modern architecture has been the city, its first victim was surely the garden.

At the beginning of this century there existed a very great concern for the garden as support and extension of the house. The house was to be surrounded by a variety of enclosures and *parterres* and preferably the whole condition was not to be symmetrical, the idea being rather a symmetry of local episode associated with a general randomness supposed to be justifiable as accommodation of functional or topographical contingency.

It is in such terms that one might interpret many of the architectural/horticultural compositions of Frank Lloyd Wright, Edwin Lutyens, M. H. Baillie Scott, Charles Platt, Jacques Greber, Werner Hegemann, and others who were all of them highly concerned with what, at the Ecole des Beaux Arts, would have been designated *entourage*. This meant that, in the early years of this century, there was a widely distributed conviction that house and garden should exist in the most animated, interactive relationship. Garden was to be structure for the exhibition of house as event. Or, alternatively, house was to be event for the presentation of garden as structure. But, if about such fluctuations of reading as these we can never be sure, then, as we contemplate such an organism as Lutyens's Gray Walls at Gullane, we can scarcely be uncertain that we are in the presence of a highly constructed field from which *figure* emerges into prominence precisely because of the existence of the ground so thoughtfully provided. Which is figurative—garden or house—is, I think, immaterial. But, as we withdraw attention from Gray Walls and proceed to contemplate Gerrit Rietveld's Schroeder House at Utrecht, any ambivalence as to what is figure and what is ground evaporates. Both Gray Walls and Schroeder House are pieces of the greatest virtuosity. At Gray Walls both garden and house are, possibly, a little too tricky. Ingenuity is, maybe, a little too evident. But, at the Schroeder House, for all of its elaborate quotations from Constructivism and De Stijl, there is a complete absence of any supportive apparatus or enframing field. One might have hoped for a few cedars of Lebanon in the style of John Claudius Loudon (faint and hyper-English hope!); but even these are not provided. Instead, one discovers the paradigmatic modern architecture piece; belligerent, isolated, responsive only to the most abstract of contexts, not at all responsive to local contingency, but quite excessively so to what are presumed to be the more active contingencies of time and culture. At Gray Walls it is the spirit of the place that is the primary idea, at the Schroeder House it is the spirit of the age; and, in this shifting of criteria from *genius loci* to *Zeitgeist*,[3] it is notable that while, as object, the house becomes aggressively intensified, as space, the garden becomes correspondingly reduced to no more than a very vague tributary accessory.

Now, if the Schroeder House and Gray Walls may be considered as indicative of two states of mind, one directed toward the built solid, the other toward the unbuilt void, then the argument may proceed, from the garden to the city.

In spite of the present revival of interest in his production I am only a very reserved admirer of the architecture of Sir Edwin Lutyens; but, though most frequently I find him a little too charming, for me, his version of Hyde Park Corner will always rank among what should be considered his most celebrated performances. For I am never driven through the present absurdities of Hyde Park Corner, never observe its present degradation, without thinking both about Lutyens and about what this part of London used to be, with Park Lane emerging through Hamilton Place, the engagement of Apsley House to the general facade of Piccadilly, and then the gradual *decrescendo* into Knightsbridge. It was all without calculation; it all possessed great understatement and reserve; it all belonged to the happiest category of London accidents; it was something of almost insuperable delicacy. And now, parts of the debris of that situation, with the fatuousness inherent to bureaucrats, are ineptly entitled Duke of Wellington Place.

But, if one imagines the first Duke of Wellington revolving round and around in his tomb at what has here been executed in his name, it might now be reasonable to desert the pragmatics of the incompletely educated highway engineers for the idealist decorum and the spatial concern of Lutyens. For, simply in terms of pragmatics, the Lutyens proposal would surely have worked quite as well as the present dispensation. Indeed, could it *possibly* have worked worse? Inherently no doubt, it involved the celebration of an empire about to be lost; but, if in this area Lutyens was scarcely clairvoyant and if there were to be no more imperial celebrations, could his proposal have involved a more timid confusion which owes very much to a cynical reception of some of the precepts of modern architecture?

Perhaps comparable remarks cannot be made about the Lutyens proposal for Piccadilly Circus, for the simple reason that nothing has been done there from that date to this; and here Lutyens is perhaps a little too excited, a little too suggestive of some impossible Edwardian epiphany. However, as initial reactions cool, as one contemplates this project, one might still be disposed to wonder whether, for all its inflation, it still does not focus and exhibit some aspects of the truth of the place. No doubt it is though Lutyens were rather tired. At Hyde Park Corner we are presented with a species of hippodrome or Circus Maximus: but, if something very like this is again to be served up at the other end of the street, then one should also recognize that proposals such as these are highly provisionary. To make the Hyde Park Corner that Lutyens intimated did not really need two versions of Apsley House and two versions of Decimus Burton's screen; and, comparably, the Lutyens *idea* of Piccadilly Circus may be stripped of its profusion of palaces and still be perceived as an exceptionally suggestive exploration, intrinsically a far more pregnant proposition than any made since.

All the same, it is perhaps too literal, too less than ingenious; but, if one may imagine it being rendered susceptible to local circumstance and gaining thereby, then, to find a major piece of unbuilt London, which both grandly stipulates the ideal and elaborately engages the empirical, we must be prepared to retreat way back into the late seventeenth or early eighteenth century, to the setting which a disappointed Wren conceived for St. Paul's.

It may be a source of astonishment that this Wren project, simultaneously modest and grand, is not more acclaimed. Had it been built it would surely long ago have been advertised as among the great Baroque pieces of accommodation, a large London equivalent of such Roman miniatures as Piazza Sant' Ignazio.

No local contingency has been violated. Ludgate Hill approaches without any re-orientation. Likewise the lines of Watling Street (preceding the present Cannon Street) and Aldersgate follow their familiar traces. Comparably, the eastern trapezoid was always approximately present and the western trapezoid, a product of Ludgate Hill intended to accommodate a Hawksmoor/Vanbrugh chapter house/baptistry, is the only significant novelty. It is all enormously economical and persuasive. We accept what exists. We build from it. We also try to transcend it. The place is both the customary point of convergence which it always was and is something quite different. It is not what Wren initially wished. It is far better. The original idea of 1666, aspatial, abstract, doctrinaire—like Washington, D.C. at its worst—has experienced all sorts of empirical vicissitudes and has gained in ideal density by this experience.

Was there any possibility, after 1945, that Wren's St. Paul's Churchyard might have been realized? Theoretically, yes; practically no. Had it been presented as a possibility one might imagine a conservative and retarded consensus wishing it; but one can also imagine the defeat of any such consensus by the massed ranks of the architectural and planning intelligentsia to whom a sin against the *Zeitgeist* was, at that time, far more outrageous than any sin against the Holy Ghost. And so it is that we acquired the present bizarre setting of St. Paul's: to the east, cheap commercialism and, to the north, a labyrinthine and silly *coupe de théâtre* of the most bland and dubious state-sponsored townscape.

The prospect of what is and what might have been is embarrassing; but the accumulation of prejudices that destroyed Hyde Park Corner and vitiated the possibility of any setting for St. Paul's was, evidently, something endemic throughout the world; and if, in London, there has been no significant urban space produced during the course of the twentieth century, this should be no occasion for surprise. For, out of the whole scenario of twentieth-century urbanism, we are probably left with only one highly convincing space; and that is, strangely enough, in New York, where the tradition of space has never been elaborate and where the prevalence of object has always been extreme.

But Rockefeller Center, for all of its attenuated Art Deco externals (and probably because of these) is the only twentieth-century urban space one might dare to put into competition with spaces of the textbooks. Like Wren's setting for St. Paul's, Rockefeller Center involves both an ideal of normative procedure and an ideal of empirical concession. One supposes that the architects of Rockefeller Center were French-trained and distrusted their French training, that they had received certain restricted information as to what modern architecture was supposed to be about, but were in no sense illuminated by the so-called "findings" of Cubism, Constructivism, and De Stijl. In other words, one imagines that, in their minds, there were no fantasies about diaphanous building, no exaltations of a crystal city, no obsessions about space-time composition. And, as one looks at their details, one is obliged to observe that their stylistic ideal was not very far removed from that of the nearly contemporary Palais de Chaillot. Down below, it is all tremendously Paris 1925. Up top, it is all New York mildly subdued. But, more than this, inherently, it is a confrontation between two sorts of reason; the reason of the mind and the reason of the purse; and it is the ever-valid arguments of money which detach Rockefeller Center from its French origins, introduce the absolutely necessary empirical pressures, and render it an indisputably American piece.

Rockefeller Center is scarcely photogenic. It is apt to be dour and, architecturally, a little banal. But, as a presentation to Fifth Avenue, as a succession of highly "ordinary" spaces (the word is used in Robert Venturi's sense), as an inevitable emanation of the Manhattan grid (one should observe the very ingenious relationship to St. Patrick's across the street, the first two of the pavilions on Fifth Avenue acting to engage the church and recapitulating the theme of the two Madison Avenue pavilions flanking its apse, the other pavilions framing the axis of the Center itself, and the generally excellent "fit" of all this), as defined space below, and something quite different above, Rockefeller Center is superb and unrivalled. Therefore, while one thinks about London and also thinks about New York, one wonders how it could be that, in the one city, the proposals of

Lutyens have remained so completely unobserved, and that, in the other, a model so highly comprehensive and so very public should have existed for so long without imitations.

Object versus Context

There are many answers which may be found as responses to this problem; but the primary answer is still quite obvious. During at least the last two hundred years, academic theory has placed enormously high premia upon the building as insulated object, and from the 1920s onwards (with the disappearance of the garden?) the modern movement has been prone to follow suit: "A building is like a soap bubble. This bubble is perfect and harmonious if the breath has been evenly distributed from the inside. The exterior is the result of an interior."[4] "In contrast with frontality sanctified by a rigid static concept of life, the new architecture offers a plastic wealth of multifaceted temporal and spatial effects."[5] "Modern functional planning distinguishes itself—by dealing honestly and competently with every side, abolishing the gross distinctions between front and rear, seen and obscene, and creating structures that are harmonious in every dimension."[6]

Such are specimen illustrations of an attitude which is only too well known: Le Corbusier rather ingeniously reiterates an old and primary French argument; Theo Van Doesburg, with his "temporal" and "spatial," provides the same argument with a fashionable, post-Einsteinian and post-Cubist trim; and Lewis Mumford reiterates all this in the "concerned" voice of a "sympathetic" liberalism for which any idea of facade, any idea of necessary interface between the *res publica* and the *res privata* is a final and terrible dissimulation.

And, of course, to these illustrations of an attitude once related to intelligence there are many others which might quite well be annexed. Here one might think of Leonardo Benevolo writing in the 1960s and addressing himself to the regularities of Chester Terrace and the Rue de Rivoli: "But architectural regularity was only an expedient to give uniformity to a branch of building activity which, even here, escaped administrative control. Behind the uniform facades, individual contractors continued to work when and how they pleased, unconcerned with any comprehensive plan."[7] So much is part of a caption in Benevolo's *The Origins of Modern Town Planning;* and, as an instance of vivacious, old-time prejudice become contemporary, dull, folklore (that famous "comprehensive" with which everything is to be "integrated"!) it may stand as a significant exhibit.

However, attack upon facade and permeation of building as object can only become attack upon street: "We must kill the street! We shall truly enter into modern town planning only after we have accepted this preliminary determination," said Le Corbusier. "Against all sense the present practices [are]: *alignment on the streets and enclosed courts and light wells,* two forms entirely contrary to human well-being, and to which the Athens Charter has opposed the principle of architectural development from within to without." And, "We must destroy the impenetrable web of streets, passages, house-rows, courts . . . avenues or boulevards, enjoyed by pedestrians. Walks, traffic lanes, full of noise and smell of cars, buses motorcyles."[8] Further: "We have, of course, killed the corridor street, the street of any and every town in the world. Our dwelling houses have nothing to do with streets."[9]

It is in the context of such hysterically overstated values as these that it becomes possible to recognize and to speak of modern architecture's "object fixation" (obsessive overestimation of the built solid) and "stradaphobia" (obsessive underestimation of any linear, constructed void).

Visually oriented architects and planners abetted by callously pragmatic capitalists, all of them preoccupied with the spurious representation of an implausible public realm, had hopelessly compromised the possibilities of both decency and life; and, as the outward and visible sign of their moral hideousness, the street could only stand condemned as a disgrace to civilization, as (more or less) the psychopathic symbol of its discontents.

Naturally, in terms of so heated a critique, that there might be good streets and bad streets could scarcely be a concern; but, if the Lutyens monumental avenue from Victoria Station to Buckingham Palace might, in the framework of such a polemic, stand as a very obvious target, then it could also follow (and quite automatically) that Van Eesteren's brilliantly sober and diversified project of 1925 for the Unter den Linden would, almost like Rockefeller Center, remain scarcely a visible model. In fact, the street—often so confusing, so popular, and so necessary—was coming rapidly to be regarded as an instrument of repression; and therefore, in Berlin, where in late Weimar days the pace was so hectic, it should not be surprising that when, circa 1930, Ludwig Hilberseimer came to make a project also related to the Unter den Linden, his propensity was altogether to deny its existence.

So one contemplates the Hilberseimer proposal. It is interjected into what, at that time, was one of the most delicate areas of the city. In front of it there is Schinkel's Schauspielhaus with its two adjacent churches and, to its north, there is the great processional avenue (the city's primary virtue?) which Van Eesteren was at such pains to reinforce. But, for Hilberseimer, the monumental continuity of Unter den Linden is clearly a theater of only bad meanings and, evidently, in a better world, destined to be superseded, presumably in the name of rational, and abstract, equality; and it should be of interest that, even as late as 1961, the strategies of Hilberseimer prevailed. For an inspection of the contributions to the Berlin competition of that year will clearly illustrate that most of the competitors were still inflamed by the same *parti pris,* that for nearly all of them Unter den Linden was something to be diminished, one might almost say to be violated, by a series of flank attacks, by (again and again) an extreme preference given to the line of the Friedrichstrasse.

Now, in what way Hilberseimer's project is to be considered spatially superior to English by-law housing of the late nineteenth century may not be clear. Nor can it be clear how much more adequately its linear buildings might have been expected to service the requirement of human well-being. That it was thought to be socially benevolent there need be no doubt; but then, so also was English by-law housing which, with never very successful results, was at least conciliatory to the community of the street. However, these doubts only introduce a not very useful parenthesis. For, if what Hilberseimer presented has operated as one of the most pervasive of twentieth-century models, the time is now come to desert the *Zeilenbau* and to approach the point block.

With the point block, just as Hilberseimer selected one of the most fragile and elaborate parts of Berlin in order to make his demonstration, so Le Corbusier proposed to obliterate one of the most complex and closely detailed quarters of Paris in the interest of what he clearly conceived to be a Cartesian version of New York. In both cases there is a certain gruesome excess of conviction. But now, even more than with Hilberseimer (in whom one senses a certain Prussian doggedness and desperation), with Le Corbusier one is confronted with the vision of a completely reconstructed, "happy" society, happy but also efficient beyond any possibility of belief. For the dogma of permanent, universal "happiness," combined with universal managerial expertise, reigns predominant; but, if one knows to what horrors the dream leads, if the fantasies of Lutyens, by comparison, are beginning child's play, it must still be insisted that, between the two of them, both publishing dubious poetry which then became accepted as even more monstrous prose, Hilberseimer and Le Corbusier provided the basic paradigms against which we still wretchedly struggle.

The city as an accumulation of isolated solids in largely unmanipulated void and the new city within the city as primarily a Phoenix symbol — as an emblem of a new world superior to any previous life and therefore, physically quite discontinuous from its immediate environment — this favorite theme of modern architecture has persisted with remarkably few energetic indications of protest. Indeed, with all of its iconographic special pleading, until lately the idea of the new as largely discontinuous from any physical setting has survived among the unexamined norms of what has been widely regarded as progressive practice. In terms of such remarks it is interesting to notice that the detachment of Le Corbusier's *Plan Voisin,* its independence of any local clues or promptings, is curiously reproduced on almost the same site by the Josic, Candilis, Woods Bonne Nouvelle project of some forty-five years later.

However — not to make further commentary upon questions of physical context which, if they are scarcely yet among the everyday presumptions of practice, are still apt to have become among the platitudes of criticism — it remains to notice the very positive virtues of such proposals as the *Plan Voisin* and, doing so, to iterate some of the very defensible presuppositions of modern architecture which, otherwise, may soon be forgotten. Rational equality, light, air, movement, aspect, prospect, hygiene, recreation, a general limpidity, no confusion; all of these are among the spiritually refreshing virtues of that city of modern architecture which has been so crudely exploited and which, unhappily, can never be built. And it remains to confront this "enlightened," and somewhat eighteenth-century condition with the opposite and rather messy virtues of the traditional city, of which confluence and convergence are among the greatest benefits.

To select, not quite at random, a traditional city, Vigevano to the west-southwest of Milan illustrates how the continuous fabric of the buildings acts as a species of urban *poche* giving energy and legibility to its reciprocal condition, the structure of specific spaces; and how the inherent versatility of this fabric which, as a condition of more or less continuous and unprogrammed building, is relatively free from most of the dictates of function and is, correspondingly, available for the accommodation of all kinds of transient local uses.

But if so much is very obvious, and if such virtues are everyday more loudly acclaimed, and if the object building, when interpreted as a universal proposition, represents nothing more than a demolition of public life, it must still be suggested that neither the city of modern architecture nor the city which modern architecture hoped to supersede is likely suddenly to vanish away. They both represent important emotional, vested interests, and, recognizing their separate merits, it should not seriously be beyond human ability to facilitate their profitable intercourse. Or such could be the implication of the plan of Wiesbaden as it was around 1900 in which the city presents the spectacle of an elegant hybrid, of two complementary fields, one largely a solid equipped with local spaces, the other largely a void in which objects have been encouraged to proliferate, each of them giving value to its opposite condition.

Cause versus Cure
However, with these remarks which envisage a situation of intelligent urbanistic detente, we have somewhat begun to move away from our somewhat premature obituary of modern architecture, from our psychobiographical diagnosis, to the consideration of palliatives and prescriptions. If it is possible to agree with Le Corbusier that "between belief and doubt it is better to believe,"[10] then it might also be possible to assume that matters are not quite so desperate as they are often said to be, that neither physics envy nor *Zeitgeist* worship, object fixation nor stradaphobia is irremediable, and that an exacting analysis with a distinctly more varied diet may yet effect the cure. For, however psychically disturbed and intellectually sclerotic, the "patient" may yet recover. A few basic prescriptions

might now be proposed for modern architecture (and, by implication, contemporary urbanism):

One
In order to reduce the mental inflammation which has always demonstrated itself as moral excess and undue preoccupation with overarticulated solids, the patient should be encouraged to consult the visual evidence and the empirical constitution of the traditional city. For the purpose, what better or more obvious exhibit is there available than an overview of Rome? For here we are presented with the greater part of the story; a more or less uniform ceiling height; a dense matrix, tissue, or texture, from out of which relatively neutral field certain spaces are subtracted and certain objects are allowed to erupt; and so, in this aerial view of Rome, among spaces, we are primarily likely to be impressed by Piazza Venezia and its Mussolinian dependencies, by the decisive cut of the Corso and Via Flaminia, by Piazza Navona (if we look for it), by Piazza del Montecitorio, and, in the distance, by the great spaces to be associated with the Villa Borghese. And, in this view, objects are the reverse of anything primary. There are, of course, in the foreground the Vittoriano and a variety of quasivertical pieces (Torre Milizia, Column of Trajan) related to it; then, in the middle distance, one is able to discern (though not too well) the domes of the Gesu and of the Pantheon; and, finally, in different parts of the background, the Villa Medici leaps into prominence and the Palazzo di Giustizia emerges from a nineteenth-century grid of streets in order to make a confrontation with the river.

However, if we are now willing to descend from the airplane (which homogenizes) to a more normal elevation (which articulates), we can begin to find ourselves confronted with a profusion of objects; Santa Maria di Loreto, Santa Maria del Nome, the two towers of Piazza Venezia, the dome of the Gesu, the dome of the Chiesa Nuova, the Borrominian outfit (just what do you call it?) which rises about Sant' Ivo della Sapienza, and, in the background, the Papal superdome. And, of course, one may descend still further; and, once looking into the streets from the rooftops, one may begin to discern how certain phenomena, propounded up top as objects, ultimately relinquish any such ambition and, finally, present themselves as a mediation between object and prevailing tissue/texture. For which purposes, as illustration of the building which emerges from the texture of a vertical surface to assume the characteristics of object, Sant' Agnese in Piazza Navona could well serve as a prime instance.

But the condition to which attention is being directed in Rome may also be discriminated by two views of Canaletto's London and necessarily, the condition of London cannot be quite so condensed as that of Rome. So Canaletto's London, as we look from Somerset House toward the City, is a slightly defused, Baroque-Rococo presentation. Emphatically, the dome of St. Paul's is not the dome of St. Peter's and the different spiky pieces (mostly Wren) scarcely possess the memorability of their Roman precursor. Nevertheless, though in the Rome-London comparison certain issues are faded, muted, and lost, as one looks toward the City, one may still be astonished by the behavior of St. Paul's; and, as one looks toward Westminster, one may still wish to observe the preponderant roles of Banqueting House and Abbey. For, in both cases, and much more so in the City, there prevails the idea of ceiling (related to texture) and the contrary idea of object, protruding above this particular plateau of building and announcing itself in the style of grand, magisterial cadenza.

And something like this condition of horizontal datum, below which assertions are few and invariably circumspect, and above which plastic excitement, virtuosity, take over, is also to be illustrated in a carefully selected view of the Yale campus. Most of this is a fake of the London of Wren and Canaletto; but then, and acknowledging the fake, apart from topography, it might still be suggested that, nowadays, there are very few English views quite so "English" as this professes to be. Wren-Gibbs represented with some strange, atavistic enthusiasm? Possibly; but not to mock. Because to move from Rome to London, to New Haven, and finally, to Manhattan, is still to receive a version of the same message.

For, in Manhattan, the earlier sykscrapers (almost everything built before 1950) are still obedient to the principles observed in Rome. No doubt New York City is a vertical excess; but, until very recently, almost every skyscraper behaved approximately like Sant' Agnese in Piazza Navona. The Woolworth, the Chrysler, the Empire State buildings all behave this way. Below a certain level they are reticent and no more than street furniture; and at this level while they accommodate the street, they make no insistence. At street level they are quiet. They are not big and bold and grand. Instead, they only display what they intend to become above a certain highly calculated elevation. Below this, they are tranquil; and above this, they are disposed to be exuberant. The set piece, the celebration of object, the *fioritura,* belong up top.

All of which was both loved and hated by Le Corbusier: "In New York then I first learned to admire the Italian Renaissance . . . It is so well done that you could believe it to be genuine."[11] He admired a tightness of profile, a laconic contour, a graphic stringency, never virtues of London and none of them virtues of Paris since circa 1860. But, at the same time, while immensely excited by what he conceived to be inadvertent Cartesian values, he thought "a skyscraper should not be a coquettish plume rising straight up from the street. It is a wonderful instrument of concentration; to be placed in the midst of vast open spaces."[12] Le Corbusier was equally empathetic to what he supposed to be American turbulence, violence, dynamism: "Here the skyscraper is not an element in city planning but a banner in the sky, a fireworks rocket, an aigrette in the coiffure of a name henceforth listed in the financial Almanach de Gotha."[13]

And, infatuated with roofscapes of New York, with those versions of Mont St. Michel, those Gothic extravagances, those Trianons, those belvederes which, more often than not, are no more than the disguises of the water cisterns and the lift mechanisms, Le Corbusier was led to propose that the ground level of Manhattan should be raised so that the whole island might become simply a large version of Central Park with such poetical versions as these standing around in it.[14]

Two

But perhaps the divorce of object from texture, the results of the abrupt proclamation of object and then the attempt, out of a repertory of idealized objects, to insinuate some version of town center as structured receptacle, could not be better illustrated than by Le Corbusier's plan for St. Die and its comparison with an aerial view of the Spanish town of Vitoria. For, at Vitoria, with great simplicity, we are presented with a wholly ideal space, whose facades are entirely internal and whose external elevations appear to be little more than happenings, with a wholly enclosed environment which is yet able to accept outside pressures and to deliver further pressures of its own. At St. Die on the other hand is exhibited, as clearly as possible, the dilemma of the object-building, the space occupier attempting to operate as space definer, from which there ensues the production of a curiously unsuccessful labyrinth, in which it seems that ideas of centrality and hierarchy are simultaneously intimated and retracted and, in which, while convergence is an explicit aim, divergence is an implicit result. And the four or more faces of all the buildings at St. Die, a series of more or less futile gestures which effectively isolate each from each, are particularly interesting when viewed alongside the enclosing wall of buildings, one side smooth, the other corrugated, which is all that Vitoria offers.

So the few remaining devotees of orthodox modern architecture should be required to observe Vitoria, which is a relatively easy and (in design hours) painless solution; and, in terms of Vitoria, these same devoted persons should further be required to consider the almost equivalent constitution of the Place des Vosges. For here again, a type of inverted palace is made up of buildings bumpy on one side and smooth on the other, of buildings which mediate the opposed requirements of privacy and publicity, buildings which, with the most casual of gestures, are apt to engage external contingency but which, internally, after some slight emphasis upon their independence, only collaborate to enforce a reading of platonic void as prime figure.

This strategy, for practical purposes, is the inversion of the strategies to which we are now accustomed. The degree and intensity of such inversion is most succinctly to be explained by the comparison of a solid and void of almost identical proportions. If to illustrate prime solid, nothing will serve better than Le Corbusier's Unite, then, as an instance of the opposite and reciprocal condition, Vasari's Uffizi could scarcely be more adequate. For, if the Uffizi is Marseilles turned inside out—if it is a jelly mold for the Unite; if it is the dock for the Unite's boat—it is also void become figurative, active, and positively charged; and while the effect of Marseilles (contrary to intentions) is to endorse a private and atomized society, paradoxically, the Uffizi is much more completely a "collective" structure. While Le Corbusier presents a private and insulated building which, unambiguously, caters to a limited clientele, Vasari's model is sufficiently two-faced to accommodate a good deal more; and, urbanistically, it is far more active. A central void-figure, stable and obviously planned, with, by way of entourage, an irregular backup which may be loose and responsive to close context: a stipulation of an ideal world and an engagement of empirical circumstance; unlike the Unite, the Uffizi may be seen as reconciling themes of self-conscious order and spontaneous randomness and, while it accepts the existing, by also proclaiming the new, the Uffizi may be said to confer a value upon both new and old.[15]

Three
But, apart from suggesting to the still-surviving protagonists of modern architecture the usefulness of the Uffizi–Place des Vosges model, a further prescription which might suggest itself is the scrutiny of long, skinny buildings, the equivalent in thickness to the *Zeilenbau* structures of Hilberseimer or the *Maisons à Redents* of Le Corbusier; but, unlike these, operating rather more as special cases than as parts of a general system. Operating perhaps like parts of the Munich Residenz to discriminate certain conditions of texture or landscape; or like the Grande Galerie of the Louvre as it behaved during the eighteenth century, acting as a means of physical communication, as an instrument of field recognition, and (like the walls of the *hofgarten* at Munich), as sometimes filter and sometimes facade.

In this sequence there should also be considered, from Rome, the Palazzo del Quirinale and its extension, the improbably attenuated Manica Lunga, which might be several Unites put end to end; but which, in its engagement of the fabric of the city also acts with great decisiveness. For, while the Unite continues to enforce its object quality, the Quirinale is both object and space definer, permitting both street and garden to exert their separate and independent personalities; and the economy of the operation, all done so laconically and with such directness, may very well stand alongside the courtyard of the Palais Royale as a criticism of present-day procedures.

Four
But the courtyard of the Palais Royale, its walls a type of habitable *poche,* itself a species of secluded, urban room, might now be allowed to introduce the topic of the garden (first victim of modern architecture?) as comprising yet another prescription for the overcoming of object fixation.

Toward the end of a Thomas Cubitt lecture, Giancarlo de Carlo noted Baron

Hausmann's dismissal of a group of architects and, in their place, the substitution of the great Second Empire gardener, Alphand.[16] Alphand was presumably considered more capable than the architects. Had he, by then, already made his great book *Les Promenades de Paris,* which discloses that much covering up may be done with trees?

However, no great matter because, toward the beginning of this lecture, it was suggested that in the early 1920s the disappearance of the garden could be regarded as precursive to the later dissolution of the city. I would simply like to suggest that the garden may be regarded both as a model of the city and as a critique of the city; and that the architecture of trees, either articulating *parterres* or "amplifying" or "correcting" a particular condition, might well provide some kind of palliative for the contemporary predicament and even some kind of paradigm for the future. And, while still pursuing the topic of the garden, it should be pointed out to the patient that object fixation is of long standing and an inherited characteristic. Contemplating such buildings as the Petit Trianon, located in a lyrically English garden, and the Grand Trianon, a series of vertical planes arising from a highly constructed field and enclosing a pair of very carefully specified voids, should lead the patient to recognize that, in the Petit Trianon, with the presence of the English garden, the cult of the object is already emphatically announced.

Five

To direct attention to a situation almost exactly parallel to that just observed, two specimens of the French *hôtel particulier,* respectively from the midseventeenth and mid-eighteenth centuries, should now be considered. At Francois Mansart's Hôtel de la Vrilliere of the late 1630s, as at the Grand Trianon, solids serve as the disengagement of external spaces. The almost opposite condition prevails at the Hôtel de Ganac-Pompadour of rather more than a hundred years later, in which the *corps de logis,* rather like an incipient Petit Trianon, begins to announce itself as an independent pavilion.

Then, should a meditation upon these images not prove sufficiently revealing, the patient should be encouraged to consider the early culmination of this route from enclosed space to isolated object, to think really seriously about the contribution of modern architecture's alleged ancestors, Claude-Nicolas Ledoux and Etienne-Louis Boullee. And this may very well transpire to be the hardest part of the whole therapeutic process. For, resulting from a retarded influence of the late Emil Kaufmann, the patient has lately become very highly addicted to the supposed revolutionary content of late eighteenth-century French Neoclassicism; many of the magazines inspired by modern architecture would scarcely be able to survive without a fairly continuous literary tribute to this particular sector of history. Ledoux's salt works at Chaux and the ideal world which, in his fantasy, he constructed around it, Boullée's Monument to Newton, and such pieces as his

Chapel for the Dead alike refuse any implications of place or context and have recently come to be interpreted, much as the alleged analysis of needs and functions was formerly interpreted, as a revelation of first principles or a binding proclamation of ultimate values. Indeed, the patient has lately become dangerously apt to place such simplified Neoclassical projects as these in a curious critical setting involving semiotics, structuralism, and romantic Marxism; and should emphatically be warned that such a conflation of ideas, fashionable though it might be, can only insidiously swell any illusions about modern architecture as direct instrument of social change, which are among the immediate causes of its indisposition.

For explicit utopianism, coupled with explicit primitivism and reductionism—whether promoted by Marc-Antoine Laugier or Le Corbusier, whether sponsored by so-called science or so-called myth, at least since they have been received after the Enlightenment—have not exactly been productive of any spatial concern outside the limits of the built solid.

Not that the patient need entirely reject Ledoux; but, preoccupied as it is apt to be with such models as the Stalin Allée and the Esposizione Universale di Roma (Postmodernism and premodernism are apparently intimately connected!), it should be encouraged to avert its gaze from the linguistically abbreviated manifesto pieces and to consider instead such items as the Hôtel Guimard and the Hôtel d'Evry which, if the city may still be envisaged as a large house, might both be considered as little cities of appropriate complexity. And, finally, while still thinking in Albertian terms, it should be brought to the patient's attention that one of the greatest of miniature cities of Neoclassicism was Soane's Bank of England which, in its collisions of set pieces (various offices of the Bank corresponding to the Forum of Trajan, the Basilica of Maxentius, etc.) was both a condensed version of ancient Rome and, in a more remote fashion, almost an allegory of the mosaic of London estate structure. Then, with the image of the Bank of England firmly in mind, it should be emphasized that this Soane miniature city is of an infinitely more manifold nature, infinitely more generous, of a far more extended psychological range, than the entire repertory of contemporary French student production which is currently so much acclaimed. For to contemplate the "rationalism" of a Grand Prix project of 1798 is not exactly to anticipate any urbanistic excitement or pleasure from its enlargement.

With so much said by way of warning against the allurements of a so-called therapy prevalently described as "rational," one might now begin to conclude.

This lecture might quite well have been entitled, as I now recognize, "Object Fixation: Cause and Cure"; and the condition of what might be called "space shyness," the basic condition of twentieth-century urbanism, is all the more remarkable when we allow ourselves to consider that in no previous century has there ever been so much talk about space as in the present. And could one, there-fore, suggest that the critical use of this term has inhibited the production of the thing itself?[17]

Among the various therapies which I have proposed those which I find most credible are: the Uffizi strategy, the long skinny building game, and the reconsti-tution of the garden; but, if none these was to operate as remedial, then, needless to say, I regard a *revival* of the city as far more important than any *survival* of modern architecture. However, I also assume that, given diminished passion and increased tolerance, both survival and revival are to be considered as just pos-sible, though never to be so considered if the architect continues to insist that all buildings should be works of architecture; that all buildings grow from the in-side out; that all design should be total; and that the architect is the Messiah of the future.

As a final conclusion, the patient might consider the agreement between Mon-drian and Van Doesburg, which is the long-ago issue that inspired my own inter-est in matrix. Van Doesburg is the master of the axonometric approach, invari-ably separating figure from spatial matrix. Mondrian invariably maintains spatial matrix and figure in a reciprocal and constantly fluctuating relationship. And it is because, to my mind, the relationship of figure to matrix in *Victory Boogie Woogie* is the relationship of object to texture, solid to void, randomness to order, incident to norm, even individual to state — because *Boogie Woogie* allows figures to augment and to contract, to congeal and to dissolve, to erupt from ma-trix and to return to it again — that, in terms of the imaginary city which I have been examining, I feel compelled to cite this Mondrian performance as what I believe to be the instigation of anything useful which might have been said here.

Notes

The foregoing was originally given as part of the Thomas Cubitt Lecture Series at the Royal Institution, London, on June 18, 1979.

1. Samuel Coleridge's definition of a success-ful work of art, as that which elicits a will-ing suspension of disbelief, is probably still the best.

2. David Watkin, *Morality and Architecture* (Oxford: 1977).

3. I am indebted to Patrick Pinnell for certain observations with reference to *genius loci* versus *Zeitgeist*.

4. Le Corbusier, *Towards a New Architecture* (London: 1927), 167.

5. These sentiments are persistently apparent in Van Doesburg; and when do they first occur? In any case, in 1924, Van Doesburg expresses himself as follows: "In contrast to frontalism — arid in origin (with) a rigid, static way of life, the new architecture offers the plastic richness of an all-sided development in space and time."

6. Lewis Mumford, *The Culture of Cities* (London: 1940), 136.

7. Leonardo Benevolo, *The Origins of Mod-ern Town Planning* (Cambridge, Mass.: 1971), caption to illustrations 4 and 5.

8. Le Corbusier: these three quotations are taken from Sybil Moholy-Nagy *Matrix of Man* (New York: 1968). Moholy-Nagy did not specify their origins.

9. Le Corbusier, *Concerning Town Planning* (London: 1947), 22.

10. Stamo Papadaki, *Le Corbusier* (New York: 1948), 137. An excerpt from *Urbanisme* (*The City of Tomorrow*), Frederick Etchells, tr. (London: 1930).

11. Le Corbusier, *When the Cathedrals were White*.

12. Ibid., 51.

13. Ibid., 41.

14. The source of this quotation evades retrieval. Is it merely hearsay? Almost certainly not; and, in any case, a letter to the *New York Times* (Francis Brennan, March 31, 1978) which has lately been brought to my attention might serve to corroborate the persistence of Corbusian fantasy. The time is the early 1950s, the place is the twenty-third floor of the Time-Life building, and the relevant part of the letter reads as follows: "Peering out across Manhattan through his heavy hornrimmed spectacles, Corbu shook his head in wonder and to the best of my recollection, quietly asked: 'Have you ever imagined what a marvelous sight this island would be if one could bury it up to say, the 20th or 30th storey, put in some trees, some nice curving roads and make it all into a kind of park?' Answering himself, he went on: 'Then one could take charming little tours through a fabulous collection of architectural *folies de granduer*—late Gothic and Romanesque chapels, French châteaux, Greek temples, Zigurat towers, shrines of all sorts, even immense allegorical murals done in colorful mosaics. Ah, what an enchanting museum!' Then shaking his head again: '*Mais,* *maintenant c'est vraiment une architecture pour les pigeons.*'" The letter, entitled "The Pigeon's Gain," is primarily an oblique criticism of Philip Johnson's A T and T Building.

15. The foregoing paragraph is, rather more than less, a quotation from Colin Rowe and Fred Koetter, *Collage City* (Cambridge Mass.: 1978).

16. Giancarlo de Carlo, "The Cubitt Lecture 1978," *Architectural Association Quarterly* (10:2), 28–40.

17. It seems almost certain that space-talk made its decisive entry into the critical vocabulary of American and English architects with the publication of Siegfried Giedion's *Space Time and Architecture* in 1941, and Nikolaus Pevsner's *An Outline of European Architecture* in 1943. Certainly, before the early 1940s, English-speaking readers appear to have been relatively underexposed to the analysis of buildings in terms of space and, since then, have come to accept such analysis (Bruno Zevi, *Architecture as Space* 1957, might be an instance) as a relative commonplace; and quite possibly, if Le Corbusier may be taken as representative, something to the same effect may be said about French usage. For, while Corbu's earlier publications seem to be distinctly "dumb" as regard space-talk, with him too the new critical vocabulary ("ineffable space") seems to insinuate itself during the course of the 1940s and to become explicity advertised in *New World as Space* 1948.

City and Suburb in Fascist Italy: Rome 1922–43

Diane Ghirardo

When Benito Mussolini came to power in 1922, the flight of Italian farmers from the countryside to the cities was an established pattern.[1] From the late nineteenth century onward, the rural population of the new Italian state diminished, with emigration to North and South America, and internally to the promise of employment in more prosperous Italian cities. The enduring and serious depression in agriculture forced a population that normally preferred to stay home to seek survival overseas or elsewhere in Italy. Typically uneducated and extremely poor, rural immigrants were not welcomed by the residents and citizens of cities such as Turin, Milan and Rome. In the early stages of planning how to outfit Rome as a capital city, government officials took a hard line against allowing the establishment of heavy industry, on the grounds that industrial development would inevitably necessitate a large industrial working class. In public declarations, the argument in support of this decision was that the capital city should remain bourgeois, decorous and refined; but in fact, fear of the revolutionary potential of the working class — fueled by knowledge of the Paris Commune in 1871 and of strikes and urban unrest in England and elsewhere — underlay the decision to keep Rome free of industry.[2] Nonetheless, Italian cities grew enormously after 1870: Rome's population expanded from a couple of hundred thousand in the nineteenth century to nearly seven hundred thousand in 1921, over one million in 1931, and nearly one and one-half million in 1941.

Curtailing the industrial proletariat was not possible in the centers of heavy industry in northern Italy, such as Turin, where the major automobile manufacturer, Fiat, employed huge numbers of workers, or in the Mediterranean port of Genoa, where imports and exports passing through the port swelled the workforce after the unification of Italy in 1871. The workers who populated Italy's industrial centers struck fear in the hearts of the aristocracy, the new industrialists, and traditional elites loath to grant power to people they considered unworthy, uneducated, and potentially rebellious — peasants, farmers, workers. But the painful fact was that while industry needed workers in order to produce, and Italy needed industrial development in order to modernize on a par with other Euro-

Fig. 5.1. Marcello Piacentini, office building at the end of Via Bissolati, initiated in 1931. Mural depicting Rome (the she-wolf) as the fruition of a collaboration between history, agriculture, and industry—although the symbolic importance of industry over the other two is clear. Photo: Ferruccio Trabalzi.

50
Diane Ghirardo

pean nations, the political class would have to tolerate, however grudgingly, the number of workers necessary to keep the factories producing. Political motives underlay this attitude, but other concerns also figured: the infrastructures and services necessary for the new masses simply did not exist, and a consequent increase in filth, disease, and crime from overcrowding was all too common, as well as the risk that more people than jobs would converge in the cities. Anti-urban sentiments took strong root among traditional elites, and became a hallmark of Mussolini's pronouncements throughout the entire era of Fascist control, although less prominently in the first few years than after 1929. Italian public officials wrestled with the competing demands of limiting the growth of urban centers and the need for workers in the new industries, never with a satisfactory solution.

Mussolini rode to power on a wave of discontent and fear of civil strife born in the wake of World War I. When violence in urban streets became the source of a widespread demand for law and order, Mussolini capitalized on the fears to achieve power as well as to exploit street violence as a key arm of Fascist policy, so Mussolini and Fascist officials knew all too well the power of restless and unhappy masses.[3] At the same time, modernization and industrialization were also essential if Mussolini's political ambitions for a strong Italian state were to be realized. As a consequence, the Fascist government pursued apparently inconsistent policies: shifting the poor out of urban areas by moving them to the periphery in low-cost, government-built housing; restricting movement between cities and regions by instituting demographic controls in the form of registration procedures; subsidizing housing for the middle classes in urban areas; and supporting strict controls of labor in order to favor industrial development. On the whole, however, Fascist policies penalized agriculture: the politics of prices and credit favored the capital accumulation of a few large financial groups, and inevitably this increased immigration into Italian cities.

The fundamental ambivalence of Fascist attitudes toward the city, with its complex mixture of agendas, emerges clearly not only in the contradictory statements of officials and in regime propaganda, but in the cities themselves, as they were built *ex novo* or restructured under the auspices of the Fascist state. Although most Italian cities give evidence of Fascist urban policies, the urban transformations wrought in Rome, capital of Italy and arguably the most historically significant city in the country, provide some of the most compelling evidence of the developing Fascist conception of the city.[4] How were conflicting interests worked out in practice in Rome, and what were the distinguishing characteristics of the urban interventions and new suburban enclaves? Three significant strategies characterized the Fascist regime's interventions in the city of Rome: suburban development, urban restructuring in the historic center, and the construction of new centers on the periphery of the city.

Suburban Development
In 1870, when the new Savoy monarchy named it the capital of Italy, Rome's urban fabric occupied only a small part of the area inside the ancient Aurelian walls; villas, vineyards and pastures filled out the rest of the city and often concealed ruins of Roman antiquity. Wild speculation in property over the next thirty years overwhelmed any efforts to rationalize development, and the unbuilt parcels of land inside the walls were quickly swallowed up by ministries, police and army barracks, upscale apartment buildings and offices. However firmly politicians held to the idea of keeping lower classes out of Rome, they came anyway, despite the lack of housing and the uncertainty of employment. Illegal settlements arose outside the walls near the main gates, along the Portuense and outside Porta Maggiore in the quarters such as San Lorenzo. By the time Mussolini came to power in October, 1922, the population had nearly tripled and showed no signs of slowing down, and the Fascist government anxiously began to develop programs for dealing with the new immigrants.

Despite the early decision to keep Rome free of industry, some minimal industrial development was nonetheless in order: a central facility for processing milk, a slaughterhouse, structures in which to store and distribute gasoline, warehouses, and similar facilities for the light industry indispensable to the swelling middle-class population of Rome. Early on, the new government selected the area around Monte Testaccio, a mound of potshards dating back to the Roman empire, south

Fig. 5.2. Porta San Paolo seen from the portico of Adalberto Libera's Aventine Post Office, 1934. Fields and villas near the Aurelian walls were asphalted over and transformed into vast thoroughfares, interspersed with occasional new monumental constructions. Photo courtesy of Francesco Garofalo.

of Porta San Paolo, as an industrial area which would also contain housing for the poorest segments of Rome's working population.[5] Roman aristocrats found the slaughterhouse too smelly to be located near their own residences or near the historic center, but perfectly appropriate for the working classes destined to be settled in the low-income housing to be called Testaccio, in a building campaign stalled since 1907 but finally completed by 1930 under the auspices of the new Fascist administration. Both of the major strategies to control the lower income segments of the population—excluding industrial development and carefully circumscribing low-income areas and light industrial zones well outside the Aurelian walls—had thus already been developed prior to the advent of Fascism. It remained for the Fascist state to further develop and consolidate these strategies in the post–World War I period. After the first years of the regime when a rhetoric in favor of grand cities predominated, as cities grew increasingly crowded by the end of the 1920s, the rhetoric and in some cases policies did an about-face and began a propaganda campaign in favor of repopulating the countryside.[6]

Whatever the intentions of the city government after 1870, urban Rome in 1922 still contained a large low-income population within the walls, concentrated in the ancient zones around the Campidoglio, Campo dei Fiori, Teatro di Marcello, and the rest of the Renaissance and medieval quarters. Interest in reserving housing in the historic center primarily for upper income groups coincided with a number of other objectives of the regime, particularly that of excavating the ruins of ancient Rome. Spurred by Corrado Ricci and Antonio Munoz—eager archaeologists for the most part indifferent to Roman history after A.D. 476—as well as by Mussolini's imperial ambitions and efforts to link his own program with ancient Roman emperors such as Caesar Augustus, houses, churches and whole blocks and quarters of Rome were leveled in order to facilitate the archaeological digs which would bring to light vast expanses of Roman ruins. Houses and apartments on the flanks of the Campidoglio, from the Aracoeli to Bocca della Verità, were demolished to make way for the Via del Mare, a wide road planned to connect the historic center with the ancient port at Ostia, and to isolate the Temple of Vesta. On the other side of the Campidoglio all the way to the Salita del Grillo, more houses fell in order to uncover Trajan's markets and the forums of Trajan, Julius Caesar, and Augustus Caesar. In these as in many other instances, the claims of traffic and archaeological curiosity far outweighed the distress of inhabitants forcibly removed from their homes to isolated, remote, and often primitive new quarters. As early as 1924, those displaced by the enormous road and archaeological enterprises were resettled far from the city center, the first groups to Acilia, a small *borgata* situated in swamps fifteen kilometers south of Rome and hastily provided with shacks for the former residents of the Forum area, and then others to subsequent borgate constructed on the edge of the city.[7]

Over the next twenty years, thousands of families and individuals packed up their belongings and were moved by the state militia to any one of a dozen new borgate, either because they lived in houses destined to be demolished to make way for new roads or excavations, or because they lived in shacks that had to be torn down in order for middle- and upper-class housing to be constructed. Under the pretext of removing them from dark, unsanitary, airless rooms into sunshine, clean air and new housing, the government rigorously pursued its policy of expropriation and resettlement. The earliest borgate, such as Acilia, San Basilio, Prenestino and Gordiani, consisted of little more than temporary huts, without sanitary facilities, running water, or any of the accoutrements normally considered necessary for a modern subdivision. During the 1930s, the buildings became more substantial, ranging from two to five stories in height and outfitted with at least minimal sanitary facilities, and architects envisioned entire little communi-

53
City and Suburb
in Fascist Italy

Fig. 5.3. Giorgio Guidi, Piazza Capacelatro, Borgata of Primavalle, 1937. With its arcades, trees, and low-density buildings, Primavalle was one of the more successful borgate, even if surrounded by three military facilities and several kilometers from the center of Rome. Photo: Ferruccio Trabalzi.

ties, with churches, stores, markets, and health centers—frequently planned, but rarely completed before World War II and often not until decades later. Some of the designs were quite handsome, such as that of Primavalle, and the apartments were more spacious than most of the low-income housing built later, but it is difficult to argue that these borgate were preferable to the active urban neighborhoods from which the inhabitants had been ejected.[8]

Although housing in the countryside away from the noise, crowds, and dirt of the city sounded good in theory, in practice it was quite different. For one thing, the regime constructed the borgate near military posts or police barracks in order to facilitate surveillance and control, giving some indication of the range of freedom the residents would have. Also, those displaced from the center of the city moved away from their places of employment, and found commute hours added to the workday. Often the transporation network—roads, buses—followed the opening of the borgate by several years, rendering the lives of the inhabitants much more difficult as they sought both transportation and the money to pay for it. Finally, residents had to confront less tangible problems: for example, the strong bonds of friendship and mutual assistance developed over decades in the old center of Rome were ruptured, and given the problems with transportation and remote location, it was difficult to reestablish them.

For those with money, no need to rely upon public transportation, and no worries about adding two or three hours to the workday, the suburban villa remained the pinnacle of success, with its echoes of aristocratic and ecclesiastical retreats in the hills surrounding the city. Two garden cities for the middle classes were completed during the early years of Fascism, Garbatella to the south and Aniene on the northern periphery (both begun in 1920 and both originally planned by Gustavo Giovannoni).[9] Unlike the low-income districts, both were promptly served by sewers, water, and bus lines. On the whole, housing was less dense, better built, and more attractive in the garden cities. In Garbatella, situated south of the city and for the most part destined for the lower middle class, one or two story villini were scattered throughout the slightly hilly site, dispersed along curving roads and surrounded by gardens and trees. By the late 1920s, the low density of the original nucleus of houses gave way to somewhat higher densities, but the buildings still rarely exceeded two stories, except a few buildings lining the major access roads and in a hotel designated as temporary housing for those left homeless by the demolitions in the area around the Theater of Marcellus and Piazza Argentina. From its original scheme as a suburban garden city, during the years of Fascism the quarter devolved into an urban center, complete with shops, bars, restaurants, and other urban amenities. Likewise, the architectural language of the housing changed from the rural picturesque developed by Giovannoni to one more indebted to currents of contemporary European modernism and more typical of intensive housing on the outskirts of other European cities. On the far northern boundary, the Aniene Garden City was designed for middle-class residents and offered more spacious duplexes or single family residences also set in gardens on curving, tree-lined streets. The provision of urban infrastructures such as electricity, water, sewers, and bus lines made Aniene a pole of attraction for further development, and once the vast area between Aniene and Rome had been developed, most of the picturesque villas in Aniene were torn down to make way for more intensive development. Even in the best cases of middle-income housing, then, demographic pressure eventually transformed the garden cities into fully urbanized districts, and the dream of a house and garden remained out of reach of ever larger numbers of residents.

The Historic Center
The interventions in the historic center, on the other hand, were meant to accom-

plish two tasks: to facilitate the movement of automobiles, buses and trucks, and to display the splendor of Roman antiquity, even when little more than rubble remained. Where possible, the two needs were joined. From 1924 onward, Mussolini repeated the demand that the monuments of antiquity be unearthed to stand in solitary splendor; the excavations and in some cases partial reconstruction would ineluctably link Fascism to the ancient Roman empire, its emperors, and its glory. Along with the recovery of other things Roman, such as the fasces as the principal symbol of Fascism, these moves aimed to secure Mussolini a position in a direct line of descent from Roman emperors, especially Augustus Caesar, architect of the greatest moment of the Roman Empire. In 1937 Italy celebrated the bimillennium of Augustus Caesar's birth with an enormous exhibit of everything connected to him, which included a major restoration of his tomb. An entire chunk of the city, from Via del Corso to the Tiber, between Via Tomacelli and Via della Frezza, was swept away in order to unearth the ruins of Augustus's tomb, create a spectacular new piazza surrounding it, and set up the Ara Pacis Augustae in a new building along the Tiber.[10] The demands of image and of archaeologists who insisted that monuments were best displayed free of the accretions of centuries took precedence over other concerns, and represented a pattern in other urban projects as well.

56
Diane Ghirardo

Elsewhere, the twin objectives were less easily combined. After the excavation of the Roman and Imperial forums, nearly eighty-five percent of the Imperial forums were covered over with asphalt and cement to create the new Via dell'Impero (now Via dei Fori Imperiali), and on the other side of the Campidoglio, the first tract of the Via del Mare covered over yet other antique ruins.[11] Although facilitating traffic would appear to have been the chief motive, the situation was in fact more complex. The new Via dell'Impero, for example, took off from Piazza Venezia, where Mussolini's offices and the balcony from which he addressed the citizenry were located, curved around one side of the monument to King Vittorio Emanuele, bisected the forums, continued past the Basilica of Maxentius, and terminated at the Colosseum. By slicing a direct cut through the diverse monuments of antiquity and reburying many of them beneath cement and asphalt, Mussolini symbolically acknowledged and at once claimed precedence over the works of Roman emperors. Similarly, the ruins valorized included only the grand monuments rather than the houses and infrastructures of the ancient city, just as in twentieth-century Rome the urban tissue painstakingly built up over hundreds of years was sacrificed on behalf of the isolation and glorification of monuments. Facilitating traffic only accounted for part of such urban schemes, because a road such as Via dell'Impero was also destined to be the site of grand Fascist spectacles such as parades and other events symbolizing the power and force of the regime.

Under Mussolini, Rome became an enormous construction yard in which traffic flow and isolated antique monuments at key points of the road network were crafted in order to produce suggestive settings for the events and ambitions of the

Fascist regime, and these scenographic backdrops took precedence over other demands. Mussolini operated with absolute conviction, untroubled by doubts: he disparaged dark, narrow, medieval streets as dated, picturesque holdovers from a premodern era, objects of nostalgia eminently dispensable in a modern metropolis. Although vast areas were demolished and replaced by wide roads or partially rebuilt ruins, fortunately for subsequent generations, only a fraction of the demolitions envisioned in the 1931 master plan were completed.[12] Despite the staggeringly destructive character of this plan for the historic center of Rome, it contained provisions which were strikingly innovative, including the banning of subdivisions outside the master plan, and announcing the right of the state to expropriate land for public purposes as set forth in detailed sections of the plan, to occupy it even before ministerial approval (in order to contain speculation), and to require property owners with land contiguous to areas subdivided and built up by the government to construct buildings on their own land within three years or have their land expropriated. The most innovative provision of all required property owners to pay in tax one-half the increase in value of their property directly or indirectly attributable to projects provided for in the master plan.[13] Each of these provisions attempted to address the twin problems of a housing shortage and runaway land speculation, and even if rarely fully applied, they marked a singular precedent in the relation between the collective and the individual property owner which was developed further in subsequent legislation. Specifically, the law dated August 17, 1942 concerned expropriations of land for cities, and adopted an advanced position regarding the rights of the collective in conjunction with those of the private sector.[14] As public works, low-income housing, and subsidized middle-income housing were completed on the periphery, the provision of infrastructures prompted enormous land speculation in the surrounding lands. When the city or government decided to purchase additional land, the prices had swollen precisely because of government activity. Article 18 of the 1942 law explicitly provided for expropriation of land necessary for expansion at prices that did not take account of price increases directly or indirectly due to provisions for growth outlined in communal or regional master plans. An earlier law in 1935 explicitly forbade building outside the limits of the master plan, but even though both laws remained on the books in the post–World War II period, the postwar government did not take advantage of these provisions for decades.[15]

The New Forums
In keeping with Mussolini's fascination with the works of Augustus Caesar and his desire to emulate and surpass them, four major new centers were constructed on the periphery of the city beginning in the late 1920s: a sport and athletic facility, Foro Mussolini, on the northern fringe of the city; a new and modern center for the University of Rome, the Città Universitaria, to the east of the historic center; a center dedicated to film production, Cinecittà, to the southeast along the Via Tuscolano; and a setting of an international exposition in 1942 as well as a new office, government, and residential center, Esposizione Universale di Roma

Fig. 5.4. Marcello Piacentini, Rettorato, Città Universitaria, 1932–35. In the intervening sixty years, the trees have grown and so has the amount of graffiti, posters, and automobiles. On the left is the Istituto di Fisica, by Giuseppe Pagano, and on the right, the Istituto di Chimica by Pietro Aschieri. Photo: Collection of Diane Ghirardo.

(EUR), to the southwest along the route to Ostia and the Mediterranean.[16] Each of the new forums helped direct development to the edge of the city and aimed to decentralize important activities—probably in part to free up the historic center for regime parades and spectacles. The Città Universitaria and Cinecittà both addressed equally specific needs for a city aspiring to become a world-class metropolis—advanced education and cinema production—and both were unusual and innovative in Europe of the 1930s, in part because they employed a modern architectural language and in part for the concentration of the activities in compact and modern complexes outside the historic center. Marcello Piacentini called a group of young modernist architects to work with him on the university, directly challenging the opponents of modernism such as Ugo Ojetti, who consistently polemicized against modernist public buildings. But in both Cinecittà and the university, as in many of the new quarters and housing complexes constructed in Rome, a primarily esthetic relation to the organization of public and private life thinly concealed repressed class tensions that neither the Fascist gov-

ernment nor the second Republic in the postwar period effectively attenuated.

The other two major centers differed from the university and Cinecittà especially because they became major celebrations of Fascist imperial aspirations and of the cult of Mussolini, but nonetheless all four new forums addressed primary needs of the developing national capital.[17] Foro Mussolini (now Foro Italico), designed first by Enrico Del Debbio and later by Luigi Moretti, constituted the first major installation of public buildings outside the developed urban fabric; the Foro was to be a northern gateway to the city. Begun in 1928 and only completed at the onset of World War II (although enlarged by additional facilities in the postwar period), the Foro began as a setting for instruction in physical education, athletic events, and campouts by youngsters who belonged to Fascist youth organizations, but it eventually became a celebration of the new empire that Mussolini sought to construct after the invasion and conquest of Ethiopia in 1935–36. With the dispersal of pools, courts, stadiums, and buildings across a verdant landscape,

Fig. 5.5. Enrico Del Debbio, Accademia di Educazione Fisica, in the foreground, and in the rear, his Stadium of Marble Statues. To the right beyond the stadium is the large field originally intended for massive public demonstrations and subsequently the site of the Foreign Ministry. Photo: Collection of Diane Ghirardo.

59

Fig. 5.6. Luigi Moretti, Accademia di Scherma (Casa delle Armi), 1932–35. Photo courtesy of Francesco Garofalo.

Fig. 5.7. Gaetano Minnucci, Ente EUR Building, EUR, 1937. Hidden by the shrubbery are the mosaics and fountains in front of the high portico, and likewise invisible in the entrance portico is Publio Morbiducci's huge sculptural relief celebrating the building of Rome over the centuries, giving Mussolini the place of honor as the guardian of the august tradition at eye level. The inscription celebrating Italy's imperial ambitions is only partly visible along the entablature above the portico. Photo: Diane Ghirardo.

local symmetries and diverse architectural languages, the Foro bore a typological resemblance to Hadrian's Villa east of Rome, not surprising since Luigi Moretti studied and practiced archaeology before turning to architecture. Moretti's urban plans of 1936 added a broad axial approach, Piazzale dell'Impero, to the main stadium, carpeted in mosaics and bracketed by an obelisk dedicated to Mussolini at one end and a spherical fountain at the other. The mosaics explicitly linked the major events of Fascism, such as the March on Rome in 1922, with those of Roman antiquity, emphasizing the grandeur of Fascism's imperial exploits by deploying twin rows of marble monoliths along the sides of the mosaic walkway, each inscribed with an important event or date in the history of Fascism. Among the facilities planned but never completed were a huge field for mass rallies and a covered auditorium for six thousand people, as well as an outdoor theater for three thousand. With its spectacular setting along the banks of a major curve of the Tiber River with Monte Mario in the background, the Foro as finally organized by Moretti deftly combined monumental constructions such as the famous Stadium of Marble Statues with generous landscaping and greenery. Despite the austere modernity of a building such as Moretti's Accademia della Scherma and the grandeur of the mosaic-adorned Piazzale dell'Impero, the Foro's overall presence was strikingly picturesque, almost rural, even though tennis courts, stadiums, and offices came to seem mere adjuncts to the more important celebration of Fascist accomplishments.

The largest and most ambitious center planned in Rome under Fascism was EUR (called E'42 in the prewar period), developed beginning in 1937 but only completed in the decades after World War II, and even then not entirely according to the original plans.[18] On land expropriated largely from outside the limits of the 1931 master plan, an international exposition was finally approved and traced out in 1938, outfitted with the temporary pavilions typical of international exhibitions but also with a full range of buildings destined to remain after the end of the exposition as a new office and government center. Apart from definitively setting the direction of urban expansion toward the south—not only because of EUR but also because of the transportation network developed to serve EUR and future southern expansion, including roads as well as Rome's first subway—EUR attempted to set forth a model for a modern new Fascist urbanism. The southeasterly direction derived not from well-developed arguments regarding urban planning, but rather from Mussolini's rhetorical insistence on drawing Rome closer to the ancient port at Ostia, and hence the Mediterranean: once again, imperial ambitions prevailed over other considerations. Buildings planned for the future secondary urban center included a congress hall, museums of several kinds, offices for various public agencies, a church, restaurants, a post office, and many others. Woven among the public buildings and the wide streets planned with the automobile in mind were to be extensive green zones: tree-lined streets, parks of various dimensions, and even an artificial lake, all topped by a one-hundred-meter arch designed by Adalberto Libera. Housing did not equal the public buildings in importance, but from the beginning the authorization for EUR contained comments on the significance of EUR as a key dimension of a program to relieve the housing shortage.[19] Single family homes, duplexes, and medium density housing would surround the urban core, with ample gardens and trees. The new urban core was intended to form the core of what amounted to a new town outside the old city, but for middle and upper income residents rather than lower income groups.

By now the vision of the city that animated Mussolini and the Fascist regime is clear: the poor were to be removed from the historic center to the remote periphery under the supervision of one or another police or military body, in medium to high density housing with limited services; the rich and middle-income groups would inhabit more prestigious zones well serviced by urban infrastructures; new, decentralized zones for particular functions—higher education, athletics, cinema production, offices, and government bureaucracies—were located away from the center, leaving the historic center itself to be reconceived as a repository of monuments, distinguished by the presence of the ruins and artifacts of Roman antiquity, and as a setting for the rituals and spectacles of Fascism. Green spaces and vast arteries for the movement of traffic, parades, and troops prevailed at any cost, including leveling houses, churches, and neighborhoods built up and inhabited over centuries. With the emphasis on public spaces and the city as a center of collective political activity (even if orchestrated from above under Fascism), the Rome envisioned by Mussolini represents the last gasp of the pre-

Fig. 5.8. Mussolini addressing a crowd in front of the Duomo in Milan, 1932. The city here is conceived of as a series of public spaces for grand public celebrations and mass demonstrations orchestrated by the Fascist party. Photo: Ferruccio Trabalzi, courtesy Archivio Centrale dello Stato.

modern city, in that it ignores the fundamental facts of modern life—that is, that interests and activities in the western world have shifted from the public realm to the private, with the public simply a setting for consumption. None of this figures in Mussolini's Rome: in the Fascist plans, Rome was still characterized chiefly by its public life, even if officials tried to insure that the participants did not include the lower classes and the poor.

Notes

1. Anna Treves, *Le migrazioni interne nell'Italia fascista: Politica e realtà demografica* (Turin: Einaudi, 1976); see also the reports published by the Commissariato per le migrazioni e la colonizzazione interna, *Le migrazioni interne in Italia nell'anno 1932–X* (Rome: Poligrafico dello Stato, 1933); and *Le migrazioni interne in Italia nell'anno 1934–XII* (Rome: Poligrafico dello Stato, 1935). Many of the bureaucratic procedures established under fascism in order to control the movement of the population are still in effect today; one must declare a residency, which is verified by a personal visit by a police officer to one's home, and in order to move from one city to another one must file for a change of residence in the new city and have all documents forwarded to the new city. Without a residency, one can neither open a bank account nor purchase a car, nor send one's children to school.

2. Eberhard Schroeter discussed these decisions in his article, "Rome's First National State Architecture, The Palazzo delle Finanze," in H. Millon and L. Nochlin, eds. *Art and Architecture in the Service of Politics* (Cambridge, Mass.: MIT Press, 1978), 128–49.

3. For further information on attitudes toward street violence in Fascist Italy, see my article, "Architecture and Theater: The Street in Fascist Italy," in Stephen C. Foster, ed. *"Event" Arts and Art Events* (Ann Arbor: UMI Research Press, 1988), 175–99. See also Treves, *Le migrazioni interne nell'Italia fascista.*

4. Several books provided essential background information for this article. On the urban history of Rome in the twentieth century, see: G. Accasto, V. Fraticelli, and R. Nicolini, *L'architettura di Roma capitale 1870–1970* (Rome: Edizioni Golem, 1971); Unione Romana Ingegneri e Architetti, *La Terza Roma* (Rome: Fratelli Palombi Edizioni, 1971); Italo Insolera, *Roma moderna: Un secolo di storia urbanistica 1870–1970* (Turin: Einaudi 1976); Marcello Piacentini, *Le vicende edilizie di Roma dal 1870 ad oggi* (Rome: Fratelli Palombi Edizioni, 1952).

5. Simona Lunadei provides a detailed history of Testaccio up to the onset of Fascism in *Testaccio: un quartiere popolare* (Milan: Franco Angeli, 1992).

6. Treves, *Le migrazioni interne nell'Italia fascista,* esp. chapters 1 and 2.

7. *Borgata* is a disparaging term which refers to something less than a district or a quarter, a fragment of the city detached into a rural setting without all of the infrastructures available in a city. The term dates from the Fascist period, and describes a dozen such settlements established on the fringes of the city.

8. Ferruccio Trabalzi, "Low-cost housing in Rome," in D. Ghirardo, ed. *Out of Site: A Social Criticism of Architecture* (Seattle, Wa.: Bay Press, 1991), 129–56; see esp. 137–44.

9. See Accasto, Fraticelli, and Nicolini, *L'architettura di Roma capitale,* 237–39, and 324–26.

10. Spiro Kostof provided a detailed account of this enterprise in "The Emperor and the Duce: The Planning of Piazzale Augusto Imperatore in Rome," in Millon and Nochlin, *Art and Architecture in the Service of Politics,* 270–325.

11. See Insolera, *Roma moderna,* 134.

12. Governatorato di Roma, *Piano regolatore di Rome 1931* (Milan-Rome: Treves, Treccani, Tuminelli, no date); Insolera, *Roma moderna,* 122–25; Piero Della Seta and Roberto Della Seta, *I suoli di Roma: uso e abuso del territorio nei cento anni della capital* (Rome: Editori Riuniti, 1988), 117–21. Mussolini outlined his plans for Rome in general terms on April 21, 1923, months after taking office.

13. Regio decreto legge 6 luglio 1931, n. 981; also Governatorato di Roma, *Piano regolatore.*

14. Legge urbanistica 17 agosto 1942, n. 1150. Discussions on this law are to be found in a book by one of the participants, Virgilio Testa, *Disciplina urbanistica* (Milan: Giuffrè, 1974), 30 et passim. See also Della Seta and Della Seta, *I suoli di Roma,* 111–15.

15. Legge 24 marzo 1932, n. 355, article 9.

16. Diane Ghirardo, "From Reality to Myth:

Italian Fascist Architecture in Rome," *Modulus* 21 (1992), 10–33, also for additional bibliographic information on these projects.

17. Ghirardo, "From Reality to Myth," 14–16; Enrico Valeriani, *Del Debbio* (Rome: Editalia, 1976); Mimmo Caporilli and Franco Simeoni, eds. *Il foro Italico e lo Stadio Olimpico* (Rome: Tomo Edizioni, 1991); Antonella Greco and Salvatore Santuccio, *Foro Italico* (Rome: Multigrafica, 1991).

18. Ghirardo, "From Reality to Myth," 18–21; E. Guidoni, M. Calvesi, and S. Lux, *E'42. Utopia e scenario del regime,* 2 vols. (Venice: Marsilio, 1987).

19. See for example Regio Decreto 16 giugno 1938: ". . . Considerato che il bisogno di adeguare le costruzioni allo sviluppo demografico della città corrisponde ad una necessità imprescindibile . . ."

64
Diane Ghirardo

Escaping the City: New Deal Housing and Gustave Ring's Garden Apartment Villages

6

Dennis Domer

Franklin Roosevelt's New Deal and World War II required thousands of new federal workers, and their influx transformed Washington, D.C., and its surrounding region in a few short years. While the city grew by about thirty-five percent in the decade between 1930 and 1940, the greater metropolitan area grew even faster—more than forty-five percent. The sharp difference in these growth rates indicates a disillusionment with city living in general and particularly in Washington, D.C. New Deal workers coming to Washington for the first time avoided expensive housing and the perceived problems of a rapidly growing black population in the capital by renting in Virginia and Maryland. Whites who had lived in Washington for years joined the newcomers by leaving the city for the surrounding countryside in the 1930s. Their departure became an exodus in the 1940s when the suburbs around Washington grew by sixty-one percent, compared to a twenty-one percent growth rate in the city. In 1950 these suburbs had a population of 1,469,000 people compared to 802,118 in Washington.[1]

The Regional Planning Association of America was also "in full rebellion against metropolitan centralization,"[2] and by 1925 influential architects and planners such as Clarence Stein declared pessimistically that "the city, as a place to live, breaks down miserably; that it is perpetually breaking down; and that it will continue to do so as long as the pressure of population within a limited area remains."[3] The Federal Housing Authority agreed with the planners and promoted a policy of suburbanization under Section 207 of the New Deal National Housing Act of 1934.[4]

The FHA insured new suburban housing complexes in metropolitan areas, and around Washington, D.C., they were white-only havens that sheltered families of New Deal bureaucrats from the realities of city life. Many of these complexes were garden apartment villages which represented a relatively new type of desirable housing. In Arlington County, Virginia, developers built numerous garden apartment complexes, among them Arlington Village, Barcroft Apartments, Buckingham Apartments, Colonial Village, Fillmore Gardens, Glenayr Apart-

Fig. 6.1. Arlington Village plan, *Architectural Forum,* August, 1939.

66
Dennis Domer

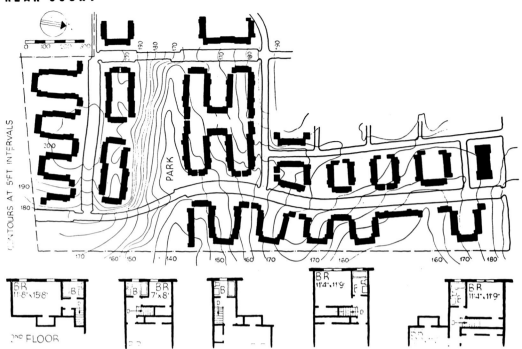

ments, Lee Gardens, Lee High Apartments, Palisade Gardens and Washington and Lee Apartments.[5] Ebenezer Howard's *Garden Cities of Tomorrow* of 1898 introduced the idea of more liveable cities protected by a green belt and separated from the central cities.[6] New complexes that made use of this idea had been built at Radburn (New Jersey, 1928), Sunnyside (Queens, New York, 1924–28), and Chatham Village (Pittsburgh, 1931). The New Deal planners of the garden apartment village used these American prototypes to develop their projects in the 1930s.

One of the most successful developers of Washington's garden apartment villages was Gustave Ring, who by 1939 held $37 million of the $100 million worth of mortgage insurance the FHA had made available for new rental housing. He was founder of the Ring Construction Company which, according to the *Washington Times,* was "one of the best known building firms in the Washington area." Ring's success depended on shrewd financing, an excellent construction organization and process, experienced architects and planners, and solid management of the complexes. Ring's Colonial Village, near Washington, is now the National Register of Historic Places, and Arlington Village, a few miles away from Colonial Village, became eligible to be registered in 1989. Furthermore, Ring made a significant profit on these enterprises. He invested about $600,000 in Arlington Village and sold it for $4 million in 1950, which represented a 666 percent profit. In 1979 Arlington Village resold for $9.7 million and is now worth perhaps $20 million.[7]

All of Ring's garden apartment villages are still very desirable, and the cost of buying condominiums in them today escalates dramatically with each turnover. Good planning, good architecture, and good management have combined to make these villages exceptional places to live. The history of Arlington Village, its developer, architecture, architect, building process, financier, occupants, and changing social structure over the last fifty years, provides valuable lessons concerning the development of future towns.

From Potato Patch to Suburb

Columbia Pike, a road which runs east-west across northern Virginia, had been a direct route to Washington since 1808, but at the beginning of the twentieth century it was still a country road about five miles from the capital city where John Hull lived.[8] An old man when he was interviewed in 1975, Hull remembered only a few country stores on the pike in 1900 such as the two-story grocery that a Mr. Terrill operated, or Siegel's store later owned by a Mr. Sher. Mostly there were small farms along the pike. Hull's maternal grandfather, Truman, owned twenty-three acres across the pike from Buckley's Woods, and there was "the Potter Farm next to Grandfather Hull's." Curtis Graham had the thirty-six acres just east of Buckley's Woods. Bertha Bradbury owned twenty-eight acres with a "little stream running through it." Miles Munson also owned twenty-eight acres west down the pike. These small farms made a bucolic playground that formed John Hull's boyhood world.

But long before John Hull's old age, this playground would be transformed into a dense suburban settlement serving a powerful world city. What were important landmarks to people who lived there in the 1920s were unimportant entities or nonexistent for the people who lived there only twenty years later. In the 1920s a contemporary of John Hull, Everett C. Norton, remembered "quite a bit of woods going back into the Army-Navy Club" where "Gus Ring bought property from B. M. Smith."[9] Charlie Sher remembered that from about 1918 "Walter Reed Drive, called Fillmore Street, had a streetcar line run by the Washington & Old Dominion Railroad," and it was the "only transportation to the district at that time."[10] But that electric train was already inconsequential for Fred Lillis thirty years later. In 1939, when Fred Lillis moved into the newly built Arlington Village, the streetcar line was still there but he and the majority of his neighbors paid the ten-cent busfare and rode to the D.C. terminus at Twelfth and Pennsylvania.[11] South Barton Street, where Fred Lillis lived, was the woods on Buckley's farm in 1920, and Lillis never even saw John Hull's favorite persimmon tree, which was a prominent feature of the site where Arlington Village would be built. It "was right in the way of the bulldozer; the first bulldozer to go in there knocked that tree down, because that was right in the middle of Barton Street."[12] Some of Buckley's woods, which once stood around the persimmon tree, had been cleared even before the March, 1939 bulldozing for Arlington Village. The site had been used as a potato field but that phase was very short-lived too.

68
Dennis Domer

The transformation of the countryside in northern Virginia between 1930 and 1950 was rapid and complete. But even before the New Dealers arrived, Washington politicians were planning for change in northern Virginia through the National Capital Park and Planning Commission, created in 1926. The commission bought land for the Mt. Vernon and George Washington parkways with funds from the Capper-Cramton Act of 1931. The NCPPC also carried out other recommendations of the 1901–1902 McMillan Plan, including new bridges over the Potomac. These new bridges, along with the automobiles using the many new roads, made John Hull's northern Virginia boyhood hills prime residential locations for white bureaucrats and businessmen who wanted to escape the problems of a racially divided, growing city. They wanted to escape but still live within a reasonable commuting distance from their offices in the monumental core of Washington. They wanted to rear their children in safe havens, and the protective qualities of the Virginia countryside would serve this need well.[13]

This great white escape is easy to document by comparing population growth rates between the city of Washington, D.C. and its metropolitan area. From 1920 to 1950 the city grew only eighty-three percent, from 453,571 to 802,178. However, the city's black population rose steadily—twenty percent between 1920 and 1930, forty percent between 1930 and 1940, and another fifty percent by 1950. The growth of the city's white population was erratic during the same thirty years— ten percent from 1920 to 1930, about thirty-three percent from 1930 to 1940, and only ten percent from 1940 to 1950. In the metropolitan area outside the city limits, however, things were different. Here, between 1920 and 1950, the population skyrocketed 179 percent from 524,469 to 1,464,089. People in the suburbs of Washington, D.C., were overwhelmingly white, and their numbers swelled particularly after World War II. In 1947 the ratio of whites to blacks in the suburbs of Washington was twelve to one. In Washington the ratio was two to one. From 1940 to 1950 Arlington County, Virginia, grew by 135 percent, Prince George's County, Maryland, grew 117 percent, and Falls Church in Fairfax County, Virginia, grew 192 percent. Many of these new suburbanites lived in "starter" garden apartment complexes such as the Colonial and Arlington Villages built by Gustave Ring.[14]

By 1939 Columbia Pike already had more of a suburban than a rural character. The pike was a macadamized road with sidewalks, and along it were gasoline stations to serve the automobiles and buses that daily carried government workers to Washington. There were also many more houses along the pike than during John Hull's boyhood, and these changes gave the land a more developed appearance with a higher population density than usually found in the country. Land prices were still relatively low, and smart investor/builders, with the support of new government housing policy, could turn the potato patches of northern Virginia into the very lucrative business of suburb building.[15]

In 1939 Gustave Ring, a young, successful Washington, D.C., businessman, bought thirty-three acres of potato patch from B. M. Smith across from the Hull house for $362,500. Instead of digging potatoes he planned to create his second FHA housing development: Arlington Village.[16] Ring knew that this part of Columbia Pike was really the Washington metropolitan area and within the ten-cent busfare circle. In relation to Washington, D.C., this potato patch could hardly be more convenient. Fred Lillis said that "Arlington Village has three things: location, location, and location."[17] Location was indeed a great boost to Arlington Village, but this would not have been enough to assure its initial or continued success.

Housing and the Ring Building Organization
The depression had made people wary and conservative with their resources. Even the new federal workers were not making very much money. Only sixty percent of them made over $150 a month, and most of them could not afford high rents. At the same time, most of these new workers had moved to Washington, D.C., from the hinterland where they were accustomed to low rents. Any new housing project for New Dealers had to be formed on the basis of an alluring price that could raise people's hopes and interests. But they wanted more than economic value.[18]

Among these hopes and interests were images of living which they had read about in popular magazines. These images often reflected the traditional American desire for a free-standing house on an ample lot. During the depression many middle-class American families simply gave up this ideal and settled for rental apartments. Chatham Village, built in Pittsburgh, Pennsylvania, in 1931–35, was a new garden apartment complex, which cast apartments into rowhouse configurations to free up as much land as possible for green, communal space and to maximize the advantages of good light and ventilation. The village advantageously used the hilly topographical features by stepping the apartment complexes to fit the curves of the land, and by trying to integrate the rowhouses sympathetically with the land. The amount of green space was increased by confining automobiles on fewer cross-streets, and building apartments tightly inside new superblocks that only the pedestrian could penetrate. Chatham Village was also a very consciously planned community. There was a market building, a park, and a communal clubhouse to help bring village life into action. Village life, as promoted by images in periodicals, seemed ideal.[19]

The concepts behind planning a neighborhood at Chatham Village, which included superblocks to eliminate cross-traffic, to separate automobiles from pedestrians, and to provide parking, were tested in 1928–29 by Clarence Stein and Henry Wright in Radburn, New Jersey.[20] Radburn and Sunnyside in New York issued from a long debate about the advantages of utopian communities, raised first in 1898 by Ebenezer Howard in *Garden Cities of Tomorrow*. Howard defined a garden city as "a town planned for industry and healthy living; of a size that makes possible a full measure of social life, but no larger; surrounded by a permanent rural belt, the whole of the land being in public ownership, or held in trust for the community."[21] Americans such as Stein, Wright, Catherine Bauer, Oskar Stonorov, Alfred Kastner, and Henry Klaber debated how to develop expressions for these utopian concepts and adapt them for public housing. For design precedents they could choose between the British picturesque, postmedieval village approach, the modern rationalism of German *Zeilenbau* design with its "International Style," or develop their own American expression based on the free-standing house tradition or the rowhouse.

This debate was fuelled by the disillusionment many intellectuals had with the congested metropolis and the chance of finding decent housing in it. The Regional Planning Association of America, established in 1923, was just as opposed to suburban diffusion as it was to urban centralization.[22] Instead, the RPAA recommended planning whole communities outside cities. The communities were to be protected by greenbelts, and in the development of the communities consideration of site, economical subdivision, superblocks, and neighborhood ambience were to have high priorities. This part of the debate was a catalyst for the flight from the city, as it occurred in Washington and elsewhere. Its message encouraged shrewd developers to erect mass housing in the countryside just outside the great cities.[23]

Gustave Ring was shrewd but he was not very interested in the theoretical issues posed by the RPAA. He was anxious to take advantage of the practical implications of planning a major housing project complete with streets, sewage and water systems, electrical and heating systems, retail services, parks, and recreation areas. Eugene Klaber and Miles Colean, from the large scale housing division of the FHA, encouraged him and pointed to provisions for community building in Section 207 of the New Deal's National Housing Act. They were convinced that Ring had enough building experience, organizational ability, financial ingenuity, and knowledge of engineering to take on such a complex task. Following the guidelines set down by the FHA and with the help of insured mortgages, he was convinced that he could cheaply construct a garden apartment with all the physical and social amenities sought by the planners. He also felt he could make a lot of money in the process. Of course, Ring wanted to make a social contribution, but his primary objective was a profitable business venture.[24]

Ring, born in Weston, West Virginia, in 1910, grew up in Washington and graduated from George Washington University with a degree in engineering.[25] He also studied architecture at night school, and then went into the construction business. His extensive projects include the Westchester Apartments in Washington; Colonial Village, Arlington Village, Brentwood Apartments, and the Marlyn Apartments in Arlington, Virginia; and the Norwood Apartments in Baltimore. In July, 1939, the FHA had $100 million of rental housing insurance, $37 million of which was developed by Ring. He was also well-known as an avid horse breeder, a board member of financial institutions, and an art collector who assembled in about forty pieces one of the best collections in Washington.[26]

By 1935, when he made his first FHA agreement to develop Colonial Village, he reportedly had built a thousand free-standing houses and was the developer of the expensive Westchester Apartments, a fully landscaped, eight-story suburban apartment complex with central management, recreational features, and services. Ring was very proud of this success, but it was Colonial Village just outside Washington in the Virginia hills that catapulted him into the national limelight. Colonial Village is a 974-unit, colonial revival apartment complex with units concentrated in modules for four families. Ring planned this development as "one harmonious and complete community," which was built in three phases between 1935 and 1937.[27] He bought fifty acres in northern Virginia distinguished by their natural beauty and short distance from Washington, and he integrated as much of that natural beauty as possible into the design of his large community. He had to build cheaply so that rooms would rent for no more than twelve and a half dollars a month each. To meet this cost standard, it was imperative that he organize the most efficient building process possible.

Ring achieved this efficiency by forming a business organization of architects, landscape architects, real estate agents, building contractors, and apartment managers. He emphasized the importance of working with persons familiar with local conditions, entrusting the planning and construction processes to specialists, developing a complete organization, and following carefully the rules of common sense in the FHA building standards. These standards focused on availability of utilities, adequate transportation, accessibility to centers of employment, stores, churches, amusements, and a low percentage of ground coverage to ensure adequate light, ventilation, and landscaping. New York Life Insurance Company held a $3,080,000 mortgage on Colonial Village, and Ring furnished about $800,000 for "land, cash funds for carrying charges and miscellaneous expense during construction, and the cash for working capital."[28]

Ring knew that this kind of building complex would be a good investment in the housing-hungry environment of New Deal Washington and would grow in value if well built, properly maintained, and fully occupied. Ring's physical and managerial organization for Colonial Village also made good sense to the housing public, who applied by the thousands for the 974 units.[29] He built on this successful investment, and he transferred his organization and concept for Colonial Village to his next project, Arlington Village. It too was a very successful and profitable venture.

Arlington Village, 1939–91
In 1939 John Sommers Hull still lived on Columbia Pike in the Sommers' house, and by that time he was employed in Arlington County as an engineer. He still knew his boyhood territory and what went on there, but he was surprised to hear that Gus Ring was going to build a 655-unit village right across the street where the persimmon tree stood and where the new South Barton Street would be cut. Hull was thankful that Ring was going to do it and not somebody else. He recalled that he was "really pleased that Mr. Ring was going to be the one to build

the Village, because I had already inspected Colonial Village over there which he built two years before. And I thought it was the best way of building apartments that I had ever seen, because it left open space. And people had a little yard to get out in . . . and most of the sections were quiet and well protected from traffic and parking places for cars."[31]

Arlington Village was the sixth FHA project built by Gustave Ring. It was designed by Harvey Warwick, a Washington architect who had designed Colonial Village. Ring furnished his organization, experience, and about $600,000 of the $2,993,000 needed to complete the project. He expected to reap an income of at least $45,000 annually from the project and pay off his investment in about thirteen years. After that Arlington Village would be his free and clear, and it would be a prime investment for years. When Ring sold it in 1950 to New England Life Insurance he had increased his original investment 666 percent. In 1979 Arlington Village resold for $9.7 million and now is worth more than twice that. Gustave Ring created a very profitable business because he knew how to build and manage a total community that people like Fred Lillis would admire and want to live in from the day Arlington Village opened on July 1, 1939.

Although Ring is reported to have bought the land for Arlington Village from B. M. Smith, the fifty-three acres that comprise the development seem to have been purchased from a number of parties. Perhaps Smith assembled the land after the 1938 survey, used part of it for his potato patch in the summer of 1938, and then sold it to Ring when the FHA deal approved the village later that year.[31]

Ring's professional organization divided the site into five superblocks, paying close attention to the sloping topography and retaining as many of the natural characteristics of the area as possible. These superblocks were delineated by South Barton Street which had to be built, South Cleveland Street which was shortened, Sixteenth Street which was lengthened, and Edgewood Street. There were 590 paved and lined parking spaces on these main streets. In the five superblocks the designers concentrated undulating strings of 661 apartments on twelve percent of the space, leaving about forty-seven acres for green space, parks, recreation areas, yards, roads, parking spaces, and service. The apartments were shaped around courts, the biggest being the "H" court flanked on the west by Thirteenth Road South, so that each apartment had a front court and a private back court. There were 357 one-bedroom, 271 two-bedroom, and 33 three-bedroom apartments, articulated individually by changing roof forms, materials, wall planes, topographical features, and a variety of simple colonial revival details.[32] The front court elevations were designed with attic medallions, varying colonial door and window surrounds, porches, shutters, gambrel roofs of slate, dormers, and careful landscaping. The back court elevations are plain and have almost no details.[33]

Fig. 6.3. Arlington Village shopping center.
Photo: Dennis Domer, 1991.

Ring reinforced the concept of Arlington Village as a community by providing a shopping center at the end of the complex on Columbia Pike. He used some of the shopping center as a rental office and central receiving area for apartment dwellers.[34] The rest he rented to various businesses for $9,600 per year.[35] He provided full maintenance and lawn service from a single maintenance center housed underneath the apartments at the corner of South Cleveland and Thirteenth Road South. There were communal facilities for washing and drying which Ring

subcontracted out to specialists. The apartments were heated by seven boiler buildings strategically placed around the village. A creek and surrounding trees were carefully preserved as a park where the children particularly liked to play.[36]

All of these design and organizational considerations helped create a sense of community at Arlington Village. Because of its size, the enclave also had "neighborhoods" which formed around the courts, and young children often concentrated their play in friendship circles determined by this court structure.[37] Children related the village to its wider community by attending neighboring public and parochial schools in Arlington County, going to movies every Saturday on the pike, and shopping with their parents at the A & P on the Pike. Fred Lillis and Virginia Smith agree that Ring's desire to build a community was realized at Arlington Village. It was and remains a comfortable, safe, and convenient place to live.

A sense of community also was forged by Ring's selection process that searched out white, middle-class citizens from among the many applicants for apartments in the village, and the narrow range of values among the villagers produced many overlapping interests and needs that were energetically reinforced by the people Ring allowed in. Ring retained his selection process until he sold the village in 1950.

The responsibility for the racist nature of Ring's selection process did not rest solely with him. It was reinforced by FHA policies, the banking system, prevailing real estate practices, and by the American people who tolerated it. The Home Owners Loan Corporation, a government agency established in 1932, applied "ethnic and racial worth to real-estate appraising on an unprecedented scale" in the judgment of Kenneth T. Jackson in his article, "The Spatial Dimensions of Social Control: Race, Ethnicity, and Government Housing Policy in the United States, 1918–1968." The HOLC assigned city blocks a real estate rating from A to D—A meaning high-income, white residential areas and D meaning that the block had, in the HOLC's assessment, "little or no value today, having suffered a tremendous decline in values due to the colored element now controlling the district." The FHA's *Underwriting Manual* of 1938 asserted that "if a neighborhood is to retain stability, it is necessary that properties shall continue to be occupied by the same social and racial classes." In 1948 Assistant FHA Commissioner W. J. Lockwood proudly proclaimed that the FHA had never insured a housing project of mixed occupancy. In his 1955 book, *Forbidden Neighbors: A Study of Prejudice in Housing,* Charles Abrams concluded that "from its inception FHA set itself up as the protector of the all-white neighborhood. It sent its agents into the field to keep Negroes and other minorities from buying houses in white neighborhoods." The FHA also seldom insured housing in a D-rated block, and this policy effectively eliminated many projects in the District of Columbia. Kenneth Jackson found that most of the FHA's commitments were in white, northwest Washington, and that "very few mortgage guarantees were issued in the predominantly black central and southeastern sections of the district." The FHA had redlined these areas and predicted in its *Washington, D.C. Housing Market Analysis* that "eventually the District will be populated by Negroes and the suburban areas in Maryland and Virginia by white families." Robert Forman in *Black Ghettos,*

White Ghettos and Slums explains that "traditional real-estate interests obtained control of the [FHA] program so that it became an extremely conservative one, tending to benefit the white suburbanite and to offer little to the dweller of the inner city." The FHA's policies had a powerful, rippling effect on real estate practices across the United States. As Forman noted, "the espousal of the restrictive covenants helped spread it throughout the country and encouraged even non-FHA property to become 'restricted' because the owner might at some future time want to be eligible for an FHA loan." The FHA finally rescinded its policy on restrictive covenants in 1949, and, in 1962, required a nondiscrimination pledge based on President John Kennedy's Executive Order 11063.[38]

It is not surprising that Gustave Ring adopted restrictive covenants for all his housing projects in northern Virginia in the 1930s. Had he done otherwise, he never would have obtained FHA insurance, and especially not in northern Virginia which the FHA had designated primarily for white, middle-class suburban development. Ring operated his racist selection process into the 1970s at Colonial Village until he was sued for racial discrimination under the Fair Housing Act. In 1973, Ring agreed to end "rental preference to persons referred by incumbent tenants" and adhere "to objective rental criteria and procedures." He also agreed to advise "representatives of the minority community" of vacancies.[39]

Ring's racial practices were good business practices, however unethical, and Ring was a very successful businessman. Above all, he was practical, and he learned from experience to repeat things that worked. Ring's experiences with his architect, Harvey Warwick, were repeatedly profitable because Warwick understood Ring's business. Warwick had designed a number of garden apartments and whole communities with Gustave Ring, including Westchester Apartments, Marlyn Apartments, Colonial Village, and Northwood Apartments. Morris Cafritz also hired Warwick to design the Park Lane, the Miramar Apartments, and the Cavalier Hotel Apartments. These were all complicated and expensive investments that shrewd businessmen could only entrust to a very competent architect.[40]

Warwick was born in Kansas City in 1893. After one year of high school at Glendale, California, he began work in his uncle John Warwick's Kansas City architectural firm in 1911. He worked there a few months, and then in 1911 began a two-year stint in the office of John Martlig where he "worked and studied day and night."[41] His next job with John Sunderland lasted from 1914 to 1915, and then Warwick moved to Duluth, Minnesota, where he was a draftsman for Edward Broomhall. Eventually Warwick became Broomhall's chief draftsman, supervising seven others, but in 1916 Warwick opened his own office in St. Cloud, Minnesota. This practice was interrupted by World War I when Warwick joined the U.S. Marine Corps. After the war Warwick moved to Washington and worked fifteen months for Edgar Mosher Concrete Engineering before he opened his own architectural firm in 1922 at 1108 Sixteenth Street Northwest.

Fig. 6.5. Arlington Village receding planes and stepped massing. Photo: Malcolm Quantrill, 1991.

When first hired by Ring, Warwick had been a practicing architect for more than fifteen years. Between 1930 and 1940 Warwick designed projects worth $14,750,000 and averaged $1,474,000 annually in work during the decade. His work dropped off during World War II because construction materials were diverted to war projects, but he still designed civilian projects worth $3,200,000 from 1941 to 1946.[42] Many of these projects were very similar, and Warwick transferred successful ideas from project to project. FHA designers liked his jux-

taposition of colonial house subtypes and the colonial revival details at Colonial Village in 1935, and these same details would be sensitively applied again to Arlington Village in 1939.

As a type, Arlington Village belongs to the rowhouse genre found so frequently in Philadelphia and many other cities on the East Coast. Apartments of various sizes, but always rectangular in shape, are connected by party walls and articulated by receding planes and stepped massing. The corner apartments have three bedrooms. The connecting modules are one- and two-bedroom duplexes with various plans, and those modules are articulated by colonial house subtypes, different materials, and different uses of colonial revival details. These expressions were not new, and that was a major advantage for it made marketing much easier. Their architectural sources lay in many well-known colonial houses on the East Coast. At Colonial Village Warwick experimented with the idea of applying colonial revival details repetitively in a garden apartment complex. Warwick found that colonial house forms worked well when collected together into rowhouses and embellished with typical, machine-made colonial details available on the market. At Arlington Village he substituted a hipped roof form for the large, end-chimney form. He also changed the apartments into thin rectangles instead of reusing the large four-family module at Colonial Village.

Fig. 6.7. Arlington Village adjusting to topography. Photo: Malcolm Quantrill, 1991.

The character of the design at Arlington Village is both picturesque and classical in nature as the horizontality of the classical cornice and attic is broken up by the picturesque verticality of gambrel, hipped and gable roofs. The cornice lines sometimes carry across different design modules, and sometimes all the horizontal connections are broken by modules which adjust up and down with the slopes of the site. Within this variety there is an overall classicizing effect which unifies the parts of the long public and private courts. This effect is produced in the balanced tradeoffs between variously expressed but repetitively used house types and colonial revival details that interact over carefully landscaped courts and walks. These repeating variations lend a sense of individuality and freedom to the apartments and at the same time manifestly insist on expressing their relationship to a larger design scheme.

This larger scheme had to meet very strict economic demands. No design was acceptable unless it could be built for $4,750 per apartment and no more than $1,1171 per room. The owner had to make money and still rent the apartments for eleven dollars a room. Building components had to be standardized, machine-made parts that bricklayers and carpenters could use easily and quickly, and in an orderly way without waste. To keep costs at a minimum, all building materials had to be purchased in bulk directly from the manufacturer. Because of the depression, labor costs were low and were decreased even further by efficient scheduling. Warwick and Ring were masters of construction as they had proved at Colonial Village.[43]

They also knew the needs of the people they wanted to move into Arlington Village, and how to provide for those needs cheaply. Warwick developed various plans to house parents with one or more children, childless couples, single persons, and old couples or widowed persons living alone. The needs of these different kinds of people and groups had to be met within small, but what were thought to be optimal room sizes at the time, and arranged in a scientifically worked out order.[44] In all configurations one entered directly into a living room leading to upstairs bedrooms and bath, and to a kitchen and connected dining room on the ground level. In the three-bedroom units, one of the bedrooms overlapped a contiguous apartment at the second floor level in order to retain the inexpensive nature of the standardized rectangular form. The apartments opened to back courts by way of the kitchen, and a special, sunken garbage disposal system was conveniently located in those back courts along the walks outside each apartment.[45] Warwick used a steam system to heat the apartments, and this system is remembered well and praised by old people who still live in the village.[46] As many systems as possible were built-in and standardized to reduce costs so that rents would not exceed eleven dollars per room, an FHA record low. All of these systems and requirements were designed to maximize light, ventilation, privacy, and open space, and to create defined circulation space which separated the pedestrian from the automobile, with parking on a few streets.

Warwick's fee for Arlington Village was $150,000 or about 6.4 percent of the total building cost.[47] This was a good fee compared to those other architects were receiving. For example, architects of defense housing projects in 1942 received a lump sum of only $48,000 on a project costing $4 million.[48] Working for Ring was good business.

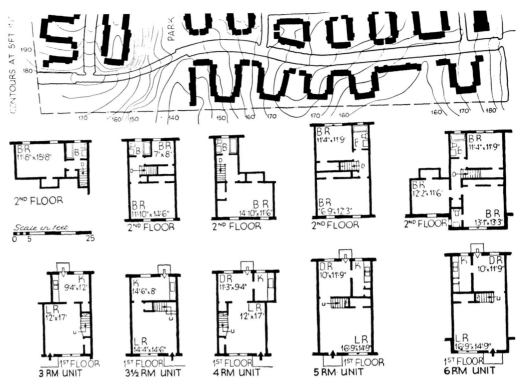

Fig. 6.8. Arlington Village apartment plans, *Architectural Forum*, August, 1939.

Standardization and simplicity keynote both the plans and exterior design of Gustave Ring's Arlington Village. Noteworthy in the floor plans for the duplex apartment units is the absence of waste space, the presence of abundant closet space; in the rear court, the absence of ornamental detail, the presence of six-family underground garbage receptacles along the central walk.

82

Dennis Domer

Besides being a shrewd businessman, Ring was a masterful contractor. He used a quick, effective, and much-admired building process that required careful coordination between the architect, the developer, and the building superintendent. John Hull thought this process was wonderful, because it saved the trees (except for the persimmon) and the little stream. Hull thought the process unique:

> [Ring would] get all of one type of work in at a time, and in proper order. All his footing men went in there and dug all the trenches for their footings . . . And then he got his plumbers in there, and they put in all the vent pipes and all the water pipes and everything . . . And then all the masons came in. And they just went to town; they really were working all over that place. And he had big, big crews working in there. It didn't take them long; they built that big village up, and he landscaped it well. He had it in good order as long as he owned it.[49]

The building process was quick. Ring got his building permit for Arlington Village on March 14, 1939. Fred Lillis moved into "H" court on July 1, 1939. Lillis reports that "H" court was built first, and then apartments were built out from the middle toward Columbia Pike. The building superintendent himself lived in one of the first apartments available so that close site supervision and coordination made the process go quickly. Continued building did not bother the new tenants.[50]

Along with a good design and an efficient building process, Ring knew that his apartments would have to be effectively managed for the investment to pay off for him and in the future for others. He set up a responsive, on-site maintenance office for the apartments and the courts. Maintenance staff kept the lawns and fixed electrical, plumbing, drainage, and other problems. They painted the interiors in a range of standard colors every three years. Tenants could select other colors, but in that case they had to buy the paint.[51] Fred Lillis, who enjoys his leisure time and doesn't want to be bothered by home repairs and lawns, summed up his forty-seven-year perspective on maintenance: "No problem!"[52]

There were indeed very few problems in the village from 1939 until the late 1960s. In those years Arlington Village was populated by white, middle-class couples who conceived their share of the large number of babies later to become the baby boomers and yuppies of the 1980s. These children filled the village, and families socialized frequently through the activities of their children. The girls went to dancing school at the shopping center for tap or ballet lessons. Boys were organized primarily around their school sports. Everyone went to the Cotillion Club on Friday nights on the pike, and the kids crossed Columbia Pike every Saturday to see movies at the Arlington Theatre. They played ball on the vacant lot on Thirteenth Road South where brick, free-standing houses were later erected. The stream in the woods had a dirt bed then, and kids played especially around a wooden bridge that crossed it. These kids, grown now, still know each other and are proud of each other's achievements.[53]

Enduring adult friendships also formed as women hung out their washes on the clothes poles in the back courts, and the men convened nightly from 8:30 to 10:30 P.M. what they affectionately called the "Senate" in the middle of "H" court.[54] Virginia Smith recalled that the Senate "knew everything and they discussed it all every night. They didn't get into personalities. They didn't gossip. They talked news. It went on for years." There was also a lot of regular "dropping in." Families took vacations together, and kids went off to camp together. It was a safe, predictable life, but its predictability rested more on natural than formal associations. There were few clubs for grownups or kids, because they weren't needed. Living closely together was enough to make the neighborhood and community work.

The close-knit community forged by depression and war experiences began to change during the 1960s. Changes in community values and standards were inevitable, and the housing planners of the 1930s and 1940s wanted their housing to accommodate change well. Henry Klaber, who worked with Gustave Ring and

Harvey Warwick from his post in government housing, subscribed to Anthony C. Wallace's opinion about the architect's responsibility to design for change: "The architect is designing the world in which a whole community is cast and has a responsibility not to allow his enthusiasm for a current (or avant garde or passe) standard of esthetic desirability to freeze the pattern of social relationships in undesirable forms for thousands of people for fifty to a hundred years to come."[55]

There is no sign at Arlington Village that its esthetic has frozen any pattern of social relationships. It is also possible that Wallace's and Klaber's view overstated the capability of design to freeze relationships in a society that is in a constant flux. Racial segregation was a much greater factor in the freezing of relationships but even that eventually broke down.

There was flux in the village in the late 1960s as American society reeled from fractious tendencies of the Viet Nam War period and from internal racial strife. Hippies and blacks lived in the village at that time, and they were decidedly not like middle-class families of the 1940s and 1950s. Virginia Smith said that "from '39 to about the mid-1960s everybody was about the same. There was no variety of colors or living styles. No unusual combinations. Then there was a phase, a not particularly good time, when a different group of people got in, and then when it went condominium, about 1979, the families were pretty much out. The kind of lower class elements were out."[56]

The social mores of this new group disturbed the conservative and protective social make-up of the village. American society as a whole was disturbed by questions raised about long hair, protests, drugs, and sex. But many hippies and blacks eventually left Arlington Village, and part of the impetus for their departure was its transformation from apartment to condominium living. This economic transformation at Arlington Village changed everything and was perhaps more effective than racial prejudice in freezing relations. After the village was converted into condominiums, it became an almost totally white, middle-class, suburban enclave. It started with a buyout.

In March, 1979 a local corporation called Arlington Village Associates bought Arlington Village from the New England Life Insurance Company for $9.7 million.[57] The buyers, including Frank S. Phillips, Preston Carruthers, Terry Eaken, and Paul Nesetta, planned to convert the apartments into condominiums. Phillips's firm would continue to manage the village as it had done since the late 1960s. Minimum disruptions, reasonable prices, and generous rebates were promised, but there was opposition among some tenants who feared they could not afford to buy. This controversy delayed the granting of a zoning variance, which would allow for the conversions, until August 1979.[58]

Much of the anxiety was assuaged when Arlington Village Associates agreed to

sell 98 units for $2.5 million to Holladay Corporation, a cooperative that leased apartments to elderly and low-income individuals. The Holladay Corporation also planned to sell some apartments for about $15,000 less than the condos.[59] These lower prices were possible because the government could lend mortgage money on them at lower rates than commercial banks. This kind of agreement was new to Arlington, and the individuals who made the agreement "became the first tenant group in Arlington, and probably in Virginia, to use this method to

Fig. 6.9. Arlington Village rear court. Photo: Dennis Domer, 1991.

85

prevent their apartments from being converted to condominiums."[60] These cooperative dwellings for less economically able people are up on the hill along Sixteenth Street in a group rather than distributed broadly in the whole of Arlington Village. The topography of the hill distinctly separates the cooperative dwellings from the condos.

When the condominiums came on the market, baby boomers bought up the rest of the village. They had plenty of money, new fancy cars, new sexual values and arrangements, and very few children. The new dwellers again are primarily white. They are single women, single women with children, married couples without children, married couples with young children, and single men. In general they are highly educated and mostly thirty to forty years old, and almost all of them work. During the day Fred Lillis is alone in his court, a different place than when he moved into this bustling village fifty years ago.[61]

There is a new "laid-back" character at Arlington Village that has replaced the enthusiastic energy of children who once set the tone and pace of village living. There is also less interaction among neighbors, who tend to lead more private lives than was possible when children drew families closely together. When these yuppies come home from work, they are too tired for children and don't need a community.[62]

Arlington Village's residents may have changed considerably since the 1960s, but its physical plant has changed very little. The colonial details and forms that face the public courts have not been altered in any significant way. The interior courts lost their sunken garbage collection system and now are filled with plastic garbage cans. In the 1960s there were extensive replacements and upgrading of kitchens and kitchen appliances. When the apartments were changed to condominiums in 1979 the steam heat was removed, and every apartment got its own heat pump for heating and cooling. Some apartments were slightly modified for the new condominium dwellers who did not want an "as is" home and therefore got new steps and new windows.[63] Some apartments got new roofs in 1981, and dozens of rear decks were built in 1983.[64] The shopping center has undergone quite a number of interior partition changes as new and different sized businesses with different needs have moved in and out.[65] In 1971 the owners put in a new swimming pool and tennis courts. To accommodate the increasing number of cars, a few of the courts lost their green space to new off-street parking.

The area around the village has changed physically, but not significantly, in the view of Fred Lillis and Virginia Smith. The pike is now a suburban strip. Fillmore Street is now Walter Reed Drive. New building is under way at South Barton and Sixteenth Street. These physical changes have not affected long-term residents like Lillis and Smith as much as the change in residents themselves. Moreover, the demographics around the village within a radius of five to six blocks have changed significantly from the former white-only composition.

Gustave Ring and Harvey Warwick could hardly have predicted in 1939 what the social and economic conditions of the United States would be like or how these conditions would affect the marketability of their garden apartments in 1991. Rather than make predictions, they considered the moment and assumed that the future, in terms of basic human needs, would not be significantly different. Ring and Warwick asked the question: what kind of housing do white people desire in the 1930s and 1940s, and how can those desires be met cheaply and with the highest quality materials possible? When they and others, especially in the Federal Housing Authority, answered that question with the garden apartment idea, Ring selected very convenient, suburban sites in northern Virginia where he built apartments to last, using relatively cheap labor and quick, efficient building methods.[66] Then Ring selected his tenants, maintained the lawns, and fixed and painted apartments regularly. For eleven years Ring made good income on Arlington Village and then he sold it for a handsome profit. It was a superb formula for becoming a millionaire.

Economics continues to be the driving force behind Arlington Village. The condominiums are still highly desirable even though they were built more than fifty years ago. They sell quickly and at escalating prices. A large part of their attraction stems from the fact that concentrating housing and freeing up land for green space produces a desirable, protected haven from the city, even though the city is not far away. Without green space and good management, the housing itself would not be so desirable and would be cheaper to buy.

The racial implications of the prevailing economics in the village remain troublesome. Race is no longer a determining factor in the selection process but the economics of that process eliminates many minorities from living anywhere in Arlington Village save in the low-income rentals. Economic factors also work against low-income whites. In spite of these realities, the architecture of Arlington Village enhances the visual integration of rental and condominium units and perhaps the social integration of the people who live there. There is an architectural egalitarianism in the village that extends to a wide range of economic and racial classes.

The concept of a garden apartment village makes sense for almost everyone in a large city. The garden apartment village responds well to the human need to establish and maintain some continuing relationship with the natural world in the middle of a concrete and noisy metropolis. Gustave Ring recognized this basic need in 1939, and he took advantage of the FHA housing policy recognizing the same need. Ring made money while his projects made good sense. This need to maintain a connection with nature has not changed since 1939 and probably will not. Villagers, now and in the future, will reap the benefits of Ring's human insight and business acumen during Roosevelt's New Deal.

Notes

This material was first presented in 1986 for Professor Richard Longstreth, who teaches American architectural history and historic preservation at George Washington University in Washington, D.C. In that year Longstreth's preservation students (I was one of them) concentrated on the string of garden apartment villages in northern Virginia. Washington, D.C. In 1987 I read a version of this paper at the ACSA national conference in Los Angeles, California, in a session entitled "The City and Its Region," moderated by Peter Papademetriou. I wish to thank James Mayo for his early reading of this material; Richard Longstreth, who recently shared all of the unpublished papers from students in his 1986 preservation class and reviewed the manuscript; William M. Tuttle, Jr., professor of history, who carefully critiqued this paper in its later stages and gave many helpful references and comments, and Malcolm Quantrill, who visited Arlington Village with me and provided photography for this publication.

1. *United States Census,* Department of Commerce, Bureau of the Census, 17th Census of the United States (Washington, D.C.: Government Printing Office, 1950). See also among the Longstreth papers Frances Alexander's "Residential Subdivisions in Arlington County," in which she traces the rapid transformation of the countryside to suburbia, and Christine M. Peleszak's "The Demographic Complexion of Arlington Virginia 1800–1950," in which she examines how the county changed from a black, poor rural area to a white, middle-class suburbia.

2. Roy Lubove, *Community Planning in the 1920s. The Contributions of the Regional Planning Association of America* (Pittsburgh: Univ. of Pittsburgh Press, 1963), 1.

3. Clarence Stein, "Dinosaur Cities," *Survey Graphic* May 7, 1925, 134–38.

4. For a general view of federal housing policy in this period see Kenneth T. Jackson, *Crabgrass Frontier: The Suburbanization of the United States* (New York: Oxford University Press, 1985), esp. the chapter entitled "Federal Subsidy and the Suburban Dream: How Washington Changed the American Housing Market." See also two Longstreth papers: Sherry Dolan, "The FHA up to 1945," and Tricia Lankester, "Housing Issues in the U.S. 1920–1941."

5. For discussions of these villages see the following Longstreth papers: Elizabeth M. Davis, "Garden Apartments in the U.S. to 1945," and "Fillmore Garden Apartments"; Francis Alexander, "Washington and Lee Apartments"; Marilyn Harper, "The Barcroft Apartments" Christine M. Pekszak, "Buckingham Community"; Stephen A. Morris, "Lee Gardens"; "Survey of Glenayr Apartments," anonymous; and "Colonial Village Nomination to the National Register of Historic Places," anonymous.

6. "Gustave Ring, builder and sportsman was 73," *Washington Times,* May 6, 1983; "Arlington Village sold to New England Mutual Life Insurance Co. of Boston," *Washington Post,* July 29, 1950; "Developers Buy Arlington Village for $9.7 million," *Washington Post,* March 1, 1979; Gustave Ring, "Building Money: The Way to Record Breaking Rents," *Architectural Forum,* August, 1939, 135–37. These figures have not been adjusted for inflation.

7. John Hull's oral history of northern Virginia is in the *Arlington Library and Zonta Club of Arlington Oral History Project* (*Arlington OHP*), interviewer Virginia L. Smith, June 20, 1975.

8. Everett C. Norton, *Arlington OHP,* Interviewer Virginia L. Smith, April 25, 1975.

9. Charlie Sher, *Arlington OHP,* interviewer Virginia L. Smith, June 10, 1975.

10. Fred Lillis and Virginia L. Smith, *Arlington OHP,* interviewer Dennis Domer, April 13, 1986.

11. Hull, *Arlington OHP,* June 20, 1975.

12. Frederick Gutheim, *The Federal City: Plans and Realities* (Washington, D.C.: Smithsonian Institution Press, 1976), 38–44; Longstreth paper: Dennis Domer, "Washington Comes of Age."

13. *United States Census,* 1950. For a discussion of the increasing segregation of Washington, D.C., see Kenesan J. Landis, *Segrega-*

tion in Washington: A Report of the National Committee on Segregation in the Nation's Capital (Washington, D.C.: National Committee on Segregation in the Nation's Capital, 1948).

14. Gustave Ring, "Large-scale Housing as a Business," *Insured Mortgage Portfolio,* 1:12 (June, 1937), 5–7, 22–24. Longstreth Papers: Stephen A. Morris, "Pre-1945 Commercial Development in Arlington County," and Marilyn Harper, "Arlington County, Va. Transportation through 1945."

15. Ring, "The Way to Record Breaking Rents," 137.

16. Lillis, *Arlington OHP.*

17. Jerome Cornfield and Marjorie Weber, "Housing of Federal Employees in the Washington Area in May 1941," *Monthly Labor Review,* November, 1941, 1236.

18. Clarence S. Stein, *Toward New Towns for America* (Cambridge, Mass.: The MIT Press, 1973), 75–86; Leland M. Roth, *A Concise History of American Architecture* (New York: Harper & Row, 1979), 266–69.

19. Roth, *History of American Architecture,* 267.

20. C. B. Purdom. "New Towns for Old: Garden Cities—What They Are and How They Work." *Survey Graphic,* May 7, 1925, 169–72.

21. Lubove, *Community Planning,* 1.

22. Eugene Henry Klaber, *Housing Design* (New York: Reinhold, 1954); Stein, *Toward New Towns for America;* Jackson, *Crabgrass Frontier*—esp. chapters entitled "Suburban Development Between the Wars," "Federal Subsidy and the Suburban Dream," and "The Cost of Good Intentions: The Ghettoization of Public Housing in the United States." See also Norton, *Arlington OHP* for comments on the developer B. M. Smith.

23. Ring, "Large-scale Housing as a Business," 5–6.

24. For biographical information about Gustave Ring, see the obituary section of the *Washington Post,* May 5, 1983, and the *Washington Times,* May 6, 1983. Also see Ring, "The Way to Record Breaking Rents."

25. "Ring 2432 Mass. Ave. N.W," *Washington Post,* August 9, 1964.

26. Ring, *Large Scale Housing,* 5.

27. Ibid.

28. Ibid.

29. Hull, *Arlington OHP.*

30. Norton, *Arlington OHP.*

31. *Apartment Development by Census Tract, 1969.* Arlington County, Virginia.

32. Most of the apartments were one-bedroom designs which would seem to fit uncomfortably with the size of the family in the 1940s and later. The average number of persons per dwelling in America in 1940 was 3.33. In 1950 the average family size was 3.37 and it fell back to 3.33 in 1960. In general, this size factor did not ever deter people from wanting to move in. However, people definitely wanted more room even in the 1940s. The U.S. Housing Census of 1950 noted that "during the past 10 years, the tendency in the housing market has been towards the creation of units of moderate size, 4- and 5-room units. Compared with the 23 percent gain in all dwelling units, 4- and 5-room units increased by 36 percent from 1940 to 1950." See *Statistical Abstracts of the United States,* 91st edition. Department of Commerce. Bureau of the Census (Washington, D.C.: Government Printing Office, 1970), 35, and *Census of Housing: 1950,* vol. I: General Characteristics, part 1: United States Summary (Washington, D.C.: Government Printing Office, 1950), xxx. David Gebhard discusses the prevalence of colonial revival in twentieth-century American architecture in his article, "The American Colonial Revival in the 1930s." *Winterthur Portfolio,* vol. 22, No. 2/3 (Summer/Autumn, 1987), 109–48.

33. Smith, *Arlington OHP.*

34. Ring, "The Way to Record Breaking Rents," 136.

35. Smith, *Arlington OHP.*

36. Ibid.

37. Kenneth T. Jackson, "The Spatial Dimensions of Social Control: Race, Ethnicity, and Government Housing Policy in the United States, 1918–1968," in Bruce M. Stave, ed., *Modern Industrial Cities* (Bev-

Escaping the City

erly Hills: Sage Publications, 1981), 79–128; Charles Abrams, *Forbidden Neighbors: A Study of Prejudice in Housing* (New York: Harper & Row, 1955); FHA *Washington, D.C. Housing Market Analysis* (Washington: FHA Division of Economics and Statistics, July 1939), 49; Robert E. Forman. *Black Ghettos, White Ghettos and Slums* (Englewood Cliffs: Prentice-Hall, 1971).

38. "Housing Suit Claims Bias against Asians," *Washington Post,* June 9, 1973, A 22 2.

39. Harvey Warwick files, American Institute of Architects Archives, Washington, D.C.

40. Warwick files.

41. Questionnaire for Architects' Roster and/or Register of Architects Qualified for Federal Public Works. May 18, 1946.

42. Ring, "Large-scale Housing"; M. H. Sugarman, "New Apartment House Design Standards," *Architectural Record.* 82:4 (October, 1937).

43. Klaber, *Housing Design.* Ring worked directly with Klaber on FHA apartments. For an earlier version of the scientific nature of apartment house design, see Sugarman's "New Apartment House Design Standards," 110ff. Sugarman, an international authority on apartment house design, outlined seven plans, minimum room sizes, room layout, appropriate coverage ratios, why tenants want and need good housing, and how they react to places like Arlington Village.

44. Smith, *Arlington OHP.*

45. Ibid.

46. Ring, "The Way to Record Breaking Rents," 137.

47. National Housing Agency Schedule of Architects' Fees for Defense Housing Projects, March 10, 1942.

48. Hull, *Arlington OHP.*

49. Lillis, *Arlington OHP.*

50. Smith, *Arlington OHP.*

51. Lillis, *Arlington OHP.*

52. Ibid.

53. Ibid.

54. Klaber. See Anthony C. Wallace, *Housing and Social Structure* (Philadelphia: Philadelphia Housing Authority, 1952). In the 1950s, the FHA wanted properties to be designed "from the viewpoint of lasting market appeal . . ." The FHA noted that "design factors leading to loss of value include, among others, the straining after picturesque effects, the use of meaningless ornamentation, a confused use of materials, the distortion of the plan to fit a preconceived notion of exterior appearance, and a desire for ostentation." See "Architectural Design under the FHA Program," *Insured Mortgage Portfolio,* Spring, 1954, 3.

55. Smith, *Arlington OHP.*

56. *Washington Post,* March 1, 1979, C6-4; *Washington Star,* February 28, 1979, A1:2; *Northern Virginia Star,* March 1, 1979; *Arlington News,* October 11, 1979.

57. "Tenants Win Zoning Delay," *Arlington Journal,* March 2, 1979, A3.

58. "Housing Pact a First." *Northern Virginia Star,* October 19, 1979, 1; "Arlington Village Tenants Form Co-op to save 98 units," *Arlington News,* October 11, 1979.

59. *Northern Virginia Star,* October 10, 1979, 1.

60. Lillis and Smith, *Arlington OHP.*

61. Ibid.

62. Smith, *Arlington OHP.*

63. Arlington Building Permits. Arlington County, Virginia.

64. Ibid.

65. The FHA insured few loans outside suburbia and very few in the District of Columbia. See Jackson, "The Spatial Dimensions of Social Control."

7

A *Wonder of the* City Beautiful *Suburbia: The* Mirabilis Suburbis *of Coral Gables, Miami*

Marco Frascari

Wonder is a metahistorical category, a particular and exceptional state of mind.[1] A cogent of mind, wonder is a sort of mental predicament marking the marvelous beginning of knowing and the end of unknowing.[2] In the construction of the human world, a mingling of esthetic thoughts and practical thoughts, wonder deals with production through a project. A category of imagination, wonder is the beginning of any project and it is always a projection of a dream. Wonder is an amazing metacategory of art production. In wonder artifacts become thaumaturgic devices and through them human life becomes urbane.

Through a mercurial and saturnine state of mind, wonder can be personified, and can be asked a key question: *How is our being presenced in the constructed world?* In other words: *How is our being in the urban world?* And as Kahn states: "Form comes from wonder. Wonder stems from our *in touchness* with how we are made. One senses that nature records the process of what it makes, so that in what it makes there is also the record of how it was made. In touch with this record we are in wonder. This wonder gives rise to knowledge. But knowledge is related to other knowledge and this relation gives a sense of order, a sense of how they interrelate in a harmony that makes all the things exist. From knowledge to sense of order we then wink at wonder and say, *How am I doing, wonder?*" (Kahn, 1986:125).

This enigmatic but poetic statement shows that in the construction of the world surrounding us, wonder is central to any intellectual and design search, since wonder is a state of desire. Wonder is a state of desire. Wonder is human desire at its beginning. An almost erotic search for understanding, for Kahn (1986:218), "Wonder is the forerunner of knowing. . . . Wonder is the primer. It primes knowing."

Wonder is a faculty that has completely disappeared from contemporary discourses on urban artifacts and it is realized only by accident in the practice of urban design. The word "wonderful" is almost meaningless, an expression of praise and celebration, used to avoid deeper and more specific comments. *It is time to restore the sense of wonder to the urban project.* Some traditional features of wonder have disappeared forever. The construction of human settlements no longer embodies the ideas of sacredness and sacrifice, of ritual rightness, of magic stability and correspondence with the universe, of perfection of form and proportion. The objective is to discover new features of wonder and to embody them in our constructed world. The work of an outstanding personality like George Merrick, a Miami developer who worked within the tradition of the "city beautiful" movement, gives us traces which must be interpreted as suggestions for how to bring the design of suburbia under the sign of wonder.

Urban formations and artifact have been sources of wonder since a direct relation was discovered between human imaginary and urban structures. Urban structures were once regarded as objects of admiration. Urban wonder is a prerational apprehension of particulars, and the details of urban artifacts — the physical expression of urban particulars — are the source of human wonderment. A story by Jorge Louis Borges, the great Argentine writer, gives us some clues to understand the powerful embodiment of wonder in urban artifacts. Borges based his story on an episode narrated by Paul the Deacon, an eleventh-century chronologist. Droctfult, a Longbard warrior, deserted to the enemy during the siege of Ravenna and died defending the city he had previously attacked. The epitaph engraved by the inhabitants of Ravenna on his tombstone indicates that Droctfult was seen not as a helpful traitor, but rather as a "visionary and a convert." Borges's wording of the explanation of Droctfult's *sub specie aeternitatis* is the first clue to understanding the peculiar and astonishing power of this city built under the sign of wonder.

> The wars bring him to Ravenna and there he sees something he has never seen, or has not seen. . . in such plenitude. He sees the day and cypresses and marble. He sees a whole that is complex and yet without disorder; he sees a city, an organism composed of statues, temples, gardens, dwellings, stairways, urns, capitals, of regular and open spaces. None of these artifacts (I know) impress him as beautiful; they move him as we might be moved today by a complex machine of whose purpose we are ignorant but in whose design we can intuit an immortal intelligence. Perhaps it is enough for him to see a single arch, with an incomprehensible inscription in eternal Roman letters. Abruptly, that revelation, the City, blinds him and renews him. He knows that in that city he will be a dog, or a child, and that he will now even begin to understand it, but that it is worth more than his gods and his sworn faith and the German marches. Droctfult deserts, and goes to fight for Ravenna (1967:171).

In this passage, the city is described as an esthetic artifact which, in order to be perceived esthetically, must be perceived as a political artifice or, better, as a thaumaturgic text accessible to a given individual according to his degree of initiation. Droctfult understood little, but his desire for knowledge moved him to

Fig. 7.1. Coral Gables, Granada entrance.

desert an economically motivated attack for a holy war. Ravenna, a thaumaturgic text like the Bible or the Koran, convinced the born warrior to engage battle in its name. In wonder everything is at stake. In our constructed world, wonder, though it can be modest in appearance, is a massive undertaking. Wonder puts people at the mercy of the constructed world. They wonder about buildings, not about themselves. We can without a doubt say that wonder is a sovereign semiotician, the royalty of meanings.

In the perception of urban texts the unity of semantic intention operates from the very beginning, when the total meaning of the text is still unknown. Every detail or particular that enters the consciousness of the observer during the act of perception is immediately evaluated in relation to its meaning. The total meaning is created by the sequence of the perception of the units. Even when all the details are not incorporated, or the total meaning of the text remains hermetic to the perceiver, the semantic unity of the text will not be invalidated. Motivation is the

93

basic requirement for the act of construction and construing. Every detail entering a text should be related to others and incorporated into the total meaning of a thaumaturgic context. Wonder is the beginning of any processes of signification. It gives buildings their meaning. It shows them to be significant; in wonder edifices do not exist for us, but we exist for edifices. As Kahn (1986:136) has stated several times, "from wonder comes realization."[3] The sense of wonder, as the root of the human desire for knowledge, should again be inserted into the constructed world through the semiotic unfolding of the mysteries of the urban and architectural disciplines.

The guide books of medieval pilgrimages demonstrate that Rome was a city built for admiration. Rome, the *caput mundi* (capital/head of the world), was the holy urban artifact of Christianity and it was *mirabilia urbis* — plentifully enriched with civic marvels — under the Christian promotion. The popes' patronage heightened the classical urban dimension of the city in one of the *mundi miracula* (miracles of the world) (Madonna, 1976:56–57).

The Latin word *mirari* means to wonder or marvel at, and *miraculum* was used in the Latin translation of the Greek version of the New Testament to indicate anything wonderful, beyond human power, and deviating from the common action of nature: a supernatural event. With a gradual change in metaphysical viewpoint, stimulated by the growth of the natural sciences, a cognate word, *admirari,* appears to have gradually acquired the meaning of a purely natural wonder, a mirror of admiration.

Marveling is rooted in the comprehension of vision and visual plays. Wonder is a mirror for carefully gazing at architectural bodies. A theoretical procedure, wonder is thus a musing which generates beautiful expressions of our understanding of how we dwell in the constructed world. Dwelling is the essence of the realization of architecture: in the design of a house was the beginning of architectural wonder. "Reflect then on what characterizes abstractly House, house, home. House is the abstract characteristic of space good to live in. House is form, in the mind of wonder it should be there without shape and dimension. A house is a conditional interpretation of these spaces. This is design" (Kahn, 1967:56).

Dwelling over the lines traced on a drawing board is the beginning of the construction of dwellings. However, before I proceed further in this wonderful "elucidation," let me dwell a little bit on the thought of dwelling. Dwelling is a very strange word. We dwell in houses, but we also dwell on thoughts. Perusing that extraordinary collection of verbal semantic semblances, the *Oxford English Dictionary,* we discover that the first definition given under the entry for the once-transitive verb "to dwell" is *to stun, to stupefy* — an obsolete meaning, of course. Consequently we make the pungent discovery, an acute perception, that in dwelling we are *stupefied*—our perception is shocked! In dwelling edifices, we are *stunned* by something which forces us to dwell in our thoughts, that is to reside in urbane buildings and edifying artifacts. A beautiful instance of the stupefying power of dwelling and its edifying utterance is in the Art Nouveau mélange of urbane buildings constituting a suburban settlement of Darmstad, the Künster-kolonie invented by the Grand Duke Ludwig von Hessen in 1899. Behind the arti-facts of this sublime suburb was the dream to construct an environment which could foster the mingling of esthetic and practical thoughts among different art-ists with differing techniques (Polano and Morello, 1989:95–96).

Wonder is a lucid dream. Wonder is the fluid which fills up the communicating vessels of the possibility and impossibility of our projects (Breton 1990). Woven into the urban fabric, wonder sets our emotions in patterns of ornate thoughts. The nature of these thoughts is revealed in the visions of wonderful theme parks such as the Monte Sacro at Varallo or the EPCOT Center in Florida, where as pilgrims we go to marvel at the miracles embodied in urban artifacts, the *sacred* wonders of the world, reduced in scale and transformed by memory.

Ut Suburbia Poiesis; A *Mardi* Parade of Dreams[4]
Throughout human history, few numbers have enjoyed the wondrous significance conferred on the number seven. Among the many groups of sevens within human lore, there are the seven Pleiades, Ptolemy's seven planets, the seven seas, the seven days of the week, the seven arts (*tirivium+quadrivium*), and, above all, the seven wonders of the ancient world, which were more than seven, but always seven. In Coral Gables, a wonderful suburb of Mediterranean nature outside of Miami, there are "seven excellent hotels" and "seven magnificent plazas." Coral Gables itself can be listed among the entries of an updated catalogue of the seven wonders.

In 1925, Miami, the "Wonder City" had began her amazing growth (Beach 1926: 13). One of the major figures behind this astonishing metropolitan occurrence was George Edgar Merrick. He arrived in Miami when he was twelve years old. His father, the Reverend Solomon G. Merrick, owned a grapefruit plantation named Coral Gables, established in 1899. Reverend Merrick died in 1911 and the young Merrick took over the estate and began expanding it; by 1912 he had ac-quired sixteen hundred acres (Wilkins, 1978:6). In 1916 Merrick married Eunice Peacock, niece of the British couple Charles and Isabella Peacock, the pioneer de-velopers of Coconut Grove. In 1920 Merrick began to plan a suburb responsive to climate, to ecological conditions, and to his vision of demonstrative urban ar-tifacts. An hybrid of Venetian and Spanish architecture, this "monstrous suburb" was planned by Merrick together with his uncle Denman Fink, a sophisticated painter of murals, and the landscape architect, Frank Button. In June, 1921, Mer-rick had the grapefruit grove removed and in December began selling the land. By 1925 this master suburb of Miami had become a chartered town.

Fig. 7.2. Coral Gables, postcard.

On the one hand, Merrick has always been judged as a shrewd businessman with an acute and creative mind. On the other hand, he has been seen as a poet who used his visionary dream to sustain his commercial acumen. Merrick's vision is seen as an expression of unusual foresight which restrained his desire "of cashing in on mouth-watering profits offered by the virtually unlimited real estate potential of the site" (Tormenter, 1989:144). This ambiguous and paradoxical duality is the fertile essence of Merrick's imaginative intuition, which transformed itself through the thoughtful design of Coral Gables around the existing Florida landscape with the insertion of carefully planned large public spaces and superb urban artifacts.

Merrick hired a large number of architects to realize his dream. Besides the designs done by the previously mentioned uncle and landscape architect, many buildings of Coral Gables were designed by Phineas E. Paist, who also held the title of supervisor of architecture, and by Paul Chalfin, who was officially the consulting architect. As presented in a promotional publication by the Coral Gables Chamber of Commerce (1928:38), the leading architects designing this wondrous suburb were seven Miami and five New York architects who worked out "the detail of the great planning of house construction." Thirteen styles were used, drawn from various regions and nations in harmony with the conception of the Mediterranean style imposed by Merrick. This Mediterranean style is a mix of Spanish, Neapolitan, and Venetian traditional detailing grafted onto American suburban dwellings. J. L. Skinner, a Miami architect, was the designer in charge of the houses composed in the Florida pioneer style. The eighteenth-century French style was designed by another Miami architect, E. A. Albright. The Persian and Neapolitan Baroque design teams were led by H. George Fink, a nephew of Denman Fink. The French cottage style design team was led by G. J. O'Reilly; the Italian country houses team by F. W. Wood. Robert Weed worked on the Italian and Dutch South African houses and Clinton MacKenzie, Marian Wyeth, John Hatton, and Mott B. Smith, all New York architects, worked on the Tangier village and bazaar, on the Persian village, on the Mexican pioneer residences, and on other theme-park housing. All this is extraordinary history but it does not tell us the true story of the design of Coral Gables, a phenomenal and beautiful master suburb of Miami.

As suggested above, this wonderful suburb is a demonstration, an urban *monster*. Urban monsters give guidance by demonstrating the way architectural production should follow (*moneo*, in the sense of *monstrare*) in making visible the invisible by *stunning* us. In the sense monstrous urban artifacts become wondrous monuments (*moneo*, in the sense of *memento*), Merrick's gateways, the Venetian pool, and the plazas are urban monsters. Inspiring the awe of urbanity, they are enigmatic signs for the realization of an urban space. Urban monsters may be in the urban artifact, or be themselves the artifact. This dual nature is revealed in myth: on one hand we have the Labyrinth, constructed to house an edifying monster, the Minotaur; on the other hand we have the enigmatic edifice of the Sphinx in Egypt. In this mythical nature the two enigmatic and basic components of Merrick's theme-park suburb are clearly defined: the powerful labyrinth layout and the enigmatic urban artifacts.

The story of this wondrous suburb is told in a small and elegant volume entitled *The Miracle of Coral Gables*. In this preciously printed suburban primer, under the penname of Rex Beach (the beach king), George Edgar Merrick tells a poetic story of a young man and his dream.[5] The story is framed in a Melville-like mode of writing. It is a voyage in a dream: "It was a 'dream past the wit of man to say what dream it was,' and he must have dreamed it at the break of day, when imagining of that sort comes true, for he was not a rich man and he had little except faith and a splendid energy to draw against, nevertheless, his plan has taken shape, his city stands reveal it" (Beach, 1926:11–12). "Castles of Spain" was name of the dream that the young Merrick had in the predawn hours while delivering fresh produce to Henry Flagler's Royal Palm Hotel in downtown Miami (Wilkins, 1978:6). Under the Florida moonlight whispering voices told Merrick not to use words to demonstrate his dreams, but to build in stone: "No! Build something more solid; make your poems live in stone. We have raised a land for you: upon the walls of our houses rear houses for men. We wrought in beauty, do you the same" (Beach, 1926:13).

Never was a location more favored for building, for most material lies underfoot (Beach, 1926:55). The stones in Coral Gables are living coral rocks quarried on the site. The quarry was then transformed into the Venetian Pool, the living heart of the suburb. The Venetian Pool, the perfect urban artifact of the urbane life, became the artistic device for delight in urbanity. This marvelous device is *mise en abyme,* which is use of an element within the work that mirrors it as whole. The "great Venetian swimming pool hollowed out of the country rock" is a play

Fig. 7.3. Coral Gables, postcard.

within the play of Coral Gables, the looking glass for the admiration of suburban life.

The soft-tinted coral walls and splendid coral gateways devised by the architects under the guidance of Merrick are a voyage beyond. In this constructed story, coral rocks and stones are analogous to what the Latin classical writer called a *vivum saxum* (unquarried living stone) or a *lapis vivus* (quarried living stone). Coral is seen as a poetic fiction, an imaginative enactment by which inanimate stones come alive and generate architecture. Coral, a soft organic stone hardened by exposure, is a building material which can be easily cut and crushed, but through the passing of time it becomes enduring and eternal. Coral, a seminal material of construction, an animal-vegetable and mineral substance, is a *quick* stone in which lasting architectural thoughts can easily be embodied; an eternal presence which allows growth, since "things will grow in . . . coral rock. . . . Capillarity will draw moisture up to the roots and they will reach down through the interstices" (Beach, 1926:55). This course of constructive and edifying events, a duration which is not of the future but of the past, is a mirror of indebtedness to a sequence of constructive events described by Herman Melville for the fabrication of the "House of the Morning," in his travel novel entitled *Mardi:* "Full five hundred moons was the palace in completing; for by some architectural arborist, its quadrangular foundation had been laid in seed-coconuts, requiring that period to sprout into pillars. In front, these were horizontally connected, by elaborately carved beams, of a scarlet hue, inserted in the vital wood; which swelling out, and overlapping, firmly secured them. The beams supported the rafter, inclining from the rear; while over the aromatic grasses covering the roof, waved the tufted tops of the Palms, green capitals to their dusky shafts" (Melville, 1990:203). The urban fabric of Coral Gables shares the same demonstrative matrix as *Mardi,* Melville's most splendid literary failure. This Miami suburb is conceived as collection of Mardian islands.

During July of 1925, Merrick introduced a startling contrast within the sparse suburban fabric of Mediterranean revival style imposed on Coral Gables. With the assistance of the American Building Corporation, he inserted in the original design a new form of suburban artifacts, the theme-villages (LaRoue and Uguccioni, 1988:13). Inserted as national islands within the Mediterranean suburbia of Coral Gables, these urban villages are one of the most ingenious legacies of the wondrous theme-park design devised by Merrick. As results of the contract between the American Building Corporation and Merrick, the Italian and the Italian country villages were built, the French eighteenth-century and Normandy villages, and the Chinese and Dutch South African villages. As in Melville's ideal coral reef, these villages together with the urban architecture of the gateways and the hotels become grotesque islands of suburban life; they are wonderful demonstrations of "suburbanity." The allegorical significance of the Mardian islands can be mapped onto the allegorical significance of the architectural artifacts composing the lonely game of Merrick, a man "who longed to create fine poems who created instead, a lovely city" (Beach, 1926:13). Many nations are demonstrated in the *Mardi* parade of islands, as they are demonstrated in Merrick's parade of national villages. The suburb Coral Gables, like *Mardi,* is an "endless search of Eden" (Milton, 1986:447), the greatest and first theme park of human history. Joseph Rykwert has masterfully dubbed this theme in his book, *Adam's House in Paradise.*

Both *Mardi* and Coral Gables are epistemological quests "for the absolute against which all societies are metaphysically measured, into a search for imagery, and language, which will reveal the conflict between the ideal and the historical actual" (Milton, 1986:447). They are both voyages and dwellings "centered on the Idealist's juncture with the ideal" (Milton, 1986:449). The equivalence is between writing and designing, between reading and dwelling. The filter is construction; the tectonic of the book and the tectonic of the suburb are analogous. Building is a process of combining different materials to generate an artificial meaning. For instance, the roof tiles of Coral Gables are old Spanish tiles brought in from Cuba, a reviving of the old Mediterranean tradition of an architecture of spoils. A rich tradition which reveals the tectonic as a combinatory art is the art of dwelling. *Mardi,* the result of combinatory writing, is to Coral Gables as Rabelais's literary efforts are to the architecture of Philibert de L'Orme. All this can be traced to one of the most influential books of architectural theory, the *Hypnerotomachia Poliphili* (Poliphilo's Strife of Love in a Dream), printed in Venice in 1499. This book tells us of a dream full of architectural vision.

In the *Hypnerotomachia Poliphili,* the dream is a hypothetical design of the unknown and thereby an important tool for acquiring knowledge; the dream is seen as a narration developed within the labyrinth of reflections between the physical and metaphysical possibilities of artifacts. This oneiric locus of reflection is the place where geometry, philosophy, and science discover their common origin or "nature,"—that is, their roots in human imagination. Dreams are the way in which myths are created. Dreams are the coral of myth construction. The dream (*sopor*) is where we learn representation because a dream is a representation of being awake. During the dream visual images are dominant and a monstrous semiosis takes place. Oneiric images show the possibility of transformation, a transformation which makes visible the invisible. A dream is a mode of production in which images can be manipulated through combinations of dimensional and scale changes, and analogies, resulting in the creation of new forms and understandings. Dreams and myth are not irrational instruments; they are the ontic tools for penetrating the rigor of reason enlightening the imaginary aspects of human thinking. Dreams are a preverbal structure, a way of thinking by using images. The conclusion of the dream is "that the thought of Coral Gables isn't new, it is so old that is novel" (Beach, 1926:53).

Notes

1. In his *Iconologia,* Cesare Ripa (1603:305) wrote, "*Meraviglia* (wonder) is a certain stupor of mind that occurs when something new (*una cosa nuova*) is represented to the senses; and the suspension of the senses in that new thing which makes man admirative and stupid."

2. For a similar definition, historically grounded in the work of the Jesuit Athanasius Kircher, see Lugli (1986).

3. The same statement is repeated several times by Kahn in his speeches: "From wonder is realization" (Kahn, 1986:95). The same assertion also appears in a well-known poem he wrote in honor of Carlo Scarpa.

4. This part of the paper is also a thank-you note to the people of the department of architecture of the University of Miami, whose willingness to listen to my words brought me thrice to the suburban wonders of Coral Gables.

5. The clues that lead me to think that Rex Beach was a pen name are the copyright owned by Merrick and a line at the bottom of page 15; other internal evidences supporting this intuition are on pages 16, 52 and 53.

References

Beach, Rex, *The Miracle of Coral Gables* (New York: Currier & Harford, 1926).

Bloom, Suzzane & Ed Hill, "Dark Wonder," *Art Forum,* Summer, 1989, 86–91.

Breton, Andre, *Communicating Vessels* (Lincoln: Univ. of Nebraska Press, 1990).

Coral Gables Chamber of Commerce, Miami, Florida, *Coral Gables* (Coral Gables: Parker, 1928).

Davis, Merel R., *Melville's Mardi* (New Haven, Conn.: Yale University Press, 1952).

Dorschner, John, "Miami 27 Cities: A Burning Pot," *Abitare* 276 (July/August, 1989).

LaRoue Jr., S. D. and E. J. Uguccioni, *Coral Gables in Postards* (Miami: Dade Heritage Trust, 1988).

Kahn, Louis I., *What Will Be Has Always Been,* R. S. Wurman, ed., (New York: Access, 1986).

Lugli, Adalgisa, "Inquiry as Collection: The Athanasius Kircher Museum in Rome," *Res* 12 (Autumn, 1986), 109–124.

Melville, Herman, *Mardi and a Voyage Thither* (Putney: Hendricks House, 1990).

Moore, Maxine, *That Lonely Game, Melville's Mardi and the Almanac* (Columbia, Mo.: Univ. of Missouri Press, 1975).

Mumford, Lewis, *The City in History: Its Origin, its Transformations and its Prospects* (Harcourt Brace Jovanovich: 1968).

Parks, Avra Moore, *Miami, the Magic City* (Tulsa, Okla.: Continental Heritage Press, 1981).

Plumepe, J. C., *Vivum Saxum, Vivi Lapides,* The Concept of Living Stone in Classical and Christian Antiquity," *Traditio,* 1945, vol. I; 1–14.

Polano, Sergio and Paolo Morello, "Mirabilia Urbis, a Wonderful History," *Art Forum,* Summer, 1989, 95–99.

Ripa, Cesare, *Iconologia overo descrizione di diverse imagini dall'antichità, e di propria invenzione* (Rome, 1603).

Sterm, Milton R., "Melville: Society and Language," in J. Bryant, ed., *A Companion to Melville Studies* (New York; Greenwood Press, 1986), 433–479.

Stern, Robert A. M., ed. *The Anglo American Suburb* (New York: St. Martin's Press, 1981).

Wilkins, Woodrow, "Coral Gables 1920's New Town," *Historic Preservation,* 30:1 (January–March, 1978), 6–10.

Camptown Vitruvius: A Guide to the Gradual Understanding of Seaside, Florida

Drexel Turner

8

Any ideal plan will stand or fall on its popular appeal.

—George Collins

It seems to me a work that almost anyone with a good head and reasonable taste could have produced—where is the wonder? The wonder is that it exists in fact, and not in talk.

—Louis Sullivan

Even in the Florida plumbed by Flagler, Ringling, Mizner, Lapidus, and Disney as the fountain of promotional dreams, Seaside gushes to prodigious effect, quite beyond what might be expected from its modest size and success as a real estate venture, settled on eighty acres of the state's most marginal, if still estimable, coastline. Seaside's professionally devised "vernacular" implantation constitutes a week-end, mostly week-out phenomenon that, despite the intrusion of time-share rents, mortgages, and maintenance fees, is packaged for public consumption with quasi-utopian earnestness. We are told in an essay by Keller Easterling reprinted in a recent, all-but-authorized monograph that ends with the names *and addresses* of everyone professionally involved (except the photographers), that Seaside is nothing less than "the beginning of a thorough reexamination of town, suburb, and region in America . . . a critique of our current method of making communities . . . by which to encourage the notion of . . . a partnership of citizens rather than consumers" so as to recapture "the magic of the small town . . . its potential to create urban 'jazz'—to allow for anarchy and variation within a rhythm and tune . . ."[1]

To improvise, if slightly off-key, from this song of itself and "urban" jazz to come: Seaside is intended as a 1980s antidote to more than two hundred years of suburban sadness, the beginnings of which were apparent even in Thomas Jefferson's notes on Virginia.[2] Conveniently bypassing Sinclair Lewis, Seaside's "neo-small town"[3] ideal embodies a densely packed, diminutively scaled nostalgia of types borrowed from Charleston, New Orleans, and other southerly points, assembled as an outpost of relative affluence on the poor man's riviera that stretches from Biloxi to Daytona Beach—territory explored with no transformational agenda by Erskine Caldwell and Frederick Barthelme, and which also suited Louis Sullivan more or less the way it was. The epigraph to Seaside's matte-gloss *vade mecum* reprises Sullivan's aversion to "white-staked lonely subdivisions" and "land agents" (the absence of which he welcomed to Biloxi Bay),[4] by appropriating the dramatic prose of Sam Shepard in high-minded opposition to "zombie architecture, owned by invisible zombies, built by zombies for the use and convenience of all other zombies. A zombie city! . . . Right where we're living now."[5] Not that many will be ever be living in Seaside or places like it. For although its status as a small wonder of American suburbanism seems assured, even in its half-built condition, Seaside's liberal provision of public space and leisurely, architect-intensive mode of development make it a very finite if winsome intimation of postzombie, postconsumerist dreams come true. Rather than acknowledge, as De Tocqueville did, that the role of the imitative arts in America is to "put the real in the place of the idea,"[6] Easterling winces at the main-chance likelihood of "imitators attempting to market the 'Seaside look'" without also incorporating the (more costly) and "more significant spatial dictates of (its 'urban') code and . . . plan diagram."[7]

Spiro Kostof has discerned in the plan of Seaside a clear but contradictory fixation: "The axes, the vistas terminating in identifiable landmarks, the tree lining of avenues are all there in two dimensions, as in a Burnham fragment. This formal urban diagram is in fact the covenant of a public realm. But though the building lines are held firm, the buildings are mostly evocative suburban residences . . . the Baroque esthetic as domesticated by the Garden City movement."[8] Seaside's analogical paternity, however, is even more diffuse. The gulffront, roadside location of its faceted, fan-shaped common acknowledges both the Vitruvian imperative: "If the city is on the sea, we should choose ground close to the harbors as the place where the forum is to be built"[9] *and* the commercial commonsense of a strip-tease along the straightaway of state highway 30-A, which Seaside's planners had first resisted, proposing to relocate the highway as a humped-back bypass pushed to the rear of the site, away from the town center.

The common and the buildings fronting onto it are intended to form the most apprehensible civic as well as commercial place in Seaside. Its general configuration and the radial avenues emanating therefrom also correspond to the disposition of the Indian settlement of Big Mound City, Florida, at the edge of the Everglades (500 B.C.–ca. 1650), even to the relative placement of the big(gest) mound inland at approximately eleven o'clock in the same location reserved at Seaside for the apsidally shaped site of the town hall/conference center. They emulate as well the wind-driven, octagonal camber of ideal city plans extracted from Vitruvius in renaissance and enlightenment translations of the *Ten Books on Architecture,* and also the faceted, fan-shaped disposition of Henry IV's project for the Porte et Place de France (Claude Chastillon and Jacques Alleaume, 1610), con-

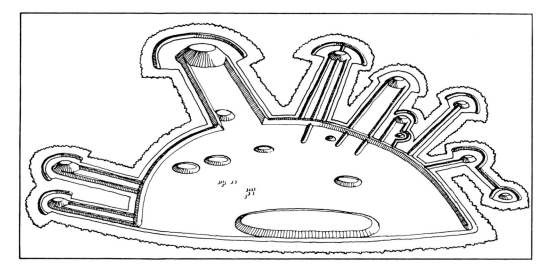

Fig. 8.1. Big Mound City, Florida, A.D. 800–1500. Based on a reconstruction by Gordon Willey. Drawing by William N. Morgan in Morgan, *Prehistoric Architecture in the Eastern United States,* MIT Press, 1980.

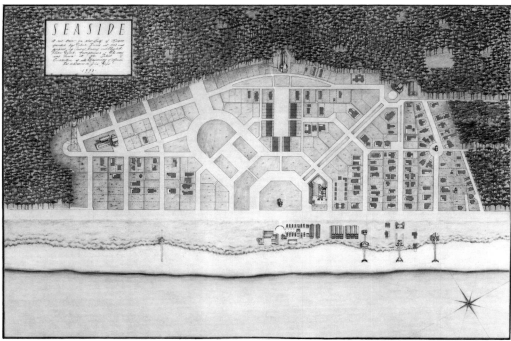

Fig. 8.2. Andres Duany and Elizabeth Plater Zyberk, Seaside, Florida (1978–83). Rendering of plan as built in 1990, but anticipating completion of Ruskin Place and Church at center top. Drawing by students at the University of Miami supervised by Francois Le Jeune.

ceived for the right bank of the Seine on the last agricultural land remaining within the walls of Paris and which retained, as at Seaside, a gardenlike pattern of development behind the ceremonial town front. In the context of postcolonial America, the essential diagram of Seaside is to be found not in John Reps's atlas but in the plan of a Virginia camp meeting ground, like that sketched by Benjamin Latrobe, 1809. But as a settlement, Seaside's scale, occasional patterns of use, and ultimate hopes for achieving sodality more closely resemble the perma-

Fig. 8.3. Clinton Avenue, Wesleyan Grove, ca. 1890. Photo from the collection of the Vineyard Museum.

nent Methodist camp towns of Martha's Vineyard and the Chautauqua settlements of New York, Ohio, and Michigan.

The hope for suburban *bienséance* in America has sometimes been supposed to require a both self-effacing and self-affirming "embodiment of a joint spirit" as postulated by Georg Simmel.[10] Such a course was suggested to Henry-Russell Hitchcock by the well-ordered, if notably austere, nineteenth-century mill villages of Rhode Island. Commending their "unusual excellence," Hitchcock speculates as to whether" . . . the salvation of American mass housing might lie in merely copying them, picket fences and all . . . we need not . . . discard our desire to emulate these villages as wholly sentimental and impractical. There is much, after all, to be learned from them. They consist of elementary and barely varied types . . . but the total effect is neither barren nor monotonous."[11] A similarly suggestive order, imbued with more decorated, gimcrack charm, is evident in the

Wesleyan Grove and Oak Bluffs camp town communities of Martha's Vineyard, where the small-scaled cottages, configured in "city-like" densities, have been endorsed by Charles Moore as "surely among the most delightsome miniatures on the face of the New World . . . a paleo-Disneyland . . . arranged in a grand plan around greenswards on which giant tabernacles . . . still stand."[12] The primmer secular reaches of Edgartown, also on Martha's Vineyard, demonstrate a similarly harmonic convergence in Moore's estimation, as "not just a collection of separate things, but something memorable in itself. It seems that in doing what he needed to do for himself, each builder also managed to do something for the whole town; the result is at once unified and energetically various . . ."[13] Partly in reproach of contemporary patterns of development, Moore ventured that although "Generations of community assent have built Edgartown; (and) Oak Bluffs came into being all at once . . . Yet it is as much a place, as memorable and special, as the one built over the centuries."[14]

Fig. 8.4. Robert Orr and Melanie Taylor, Rosewalk Court, Seaside, Florida, 1984–86. Photo: Steven Brooke.

Moore's knowing and optimistic assessment of town-making on Martha's Vineyard came while he was dean of the School of Architecture at Yale University, and while Seaside's principal planners-to-be, Andres Duany and Elizabeth Plater-Zyberk, were still students there. Also then at Yale was Vincent Scully, whose appreciation of American architecture and settlements in quasipoetic, nonheroic terms has served to acquaint several generations of students with the unobtrusive virtues of Elm Street and the amiable qualities of America's first resort architecture, which he rediscovered and named the stick and shingle styles. Historical prescience notwithstanding, Scully confesses to having "felt the existence of some strangely impassable barrier between the nineteenth-century past and the late twentieth-century present. It would never have occurred to me that the turned posts of the Stick Style could be used once again exactly as they had once been used, or that the screened porch, the most genial architectural environment ever created in the United States, could be directly revived. And though I had deplored the destruction of the traditional street and recognized the beautiful urban structure of house, lot, sidewalk, grass strip, curb, and vehicular way that had shaped most American towns, it did not seem to me that architects would ever again be able to shape that intricate urban structure."[15]

It may be debatable whether or not architects themselves really had ever been very much involved in the cultivation of Scully's everyday Eden. But as special seers, he accords Duany and Plater-Zyberk pedagogical status, recalling:

> They led me and the rest of our class through the streets of New Haven, my own city. They showed us the Stick and Shingle houses of Newport and Bar Harbor as they existed right under our noses in their everyday vernacular guise—not only as I had written about them, as objects of historical interest . . . but . . . as direct models for contemporary use. So we saw the posts and the porches anew, the wood stripping and the shingled surfaces, the frontal gables and, more than that, the front steps, the sidewalks, the grass verge with its trees—once, God help us, great elms. We saw the houses side by side, the lots narrow, the houses tall enough to shape the streets, framed and overarched by the trees. We thus saw the type, the necessary building type that can shape cities. . . . It was the type, with its beloved detailing, its decoration, that made urban order and individual variety together. It was, in the great old nineteenth-century aphorism, a matter of decorating construction, not constructing decoration. . . . Duany and Plater-Zyberk saw . . . that nothing needed to be abstracted, neither the type nor the detail. They could be used as they were. . . . Later, of course, Duany and Plater-Zyberk's own design was stiffened and simplified by the classicism of Leon Krier, but the principle remained the same, and this is their greatest accomplishment: to do it literally. This is the only way it can be done.[16]

The problem of Seaside was not only one of replicating such consensually picturesque, downhome ambience as Moore had detected on Martha's Vineyard and that Scully had been reintroduced to on the streets where he had always lived in

New Haven, but to do so according to a compressed schedule, and in the absence of any prevailing builderly entente or specially cohering sense of community purpose. It was a problem of both planning and "community architecture" in a seldom-used sense, a synthesis that Duany and Plater-Zyberk (husband and wife, he the son of Cuban emigres, she the daughter of Polish refugees) undertook beginning in 1978 in collaboration with Seaside's developer, Robert Davis, an architectural enthusiast and Harvard MBA by way of the undergraduate, young-socialist milieu of Antioch College. Davis had recently inherited the site of Seaside from his grandfather, the owner of a Birmingham, Alabama, department store, and was referred to Duany and Plater-Zyberk by an editor of *House Beautiful* magazine. Duany and Plater-Zyberk were then in the last stages of what Scully has called their "bout with Arquitectonica,"[17] the brash, salsa-fied modernism of which continues to define Don Johnson's Miami. Davis was himself engaged at that point in the development of small real estate projects in Miami with names like Apogee, which Duany characterizes as "a group of International Style town houses, very fine, especially for the time."[18]

Duany and Plater-Zyberk later also enlisted the counsel of Leon Krier, a Luxembourg-born, London-based, self-taught architect of classical—and rhetorically socialist—inclinations, whose theoretical postulations and charming, mostly utopic, urban designs they had come to consider of "fundamental importance."[19] Since 1982, coinciding with a brief residency at the University of Virginia, Krier has produced for Seaside an instructive review of the town plan (resulting in the addition of a system of pedestrian alleyways); proposals for several civic buildings (town hall/marketplace, church, and tower); and his first built work, a tempietto-topped, clapboard house for himself, completed in 1989. This last, which he calls a "sin committed in broad daylight"[20] since it contradicts his earlier, characteristically modest refusal to build at all "until I can build a city, or a piece of a city, in a way that I believe to be correct,"[21] is perhaps the best-known single building in Seaside, although Neil Levine speculates that Krier's project for an ocean-front tower for the center of the common, once built, will "no doubt make a most evocative symbol for the town . . . (and shift) the source of the view from the private to the public domain."[22]

At present, Seaside is essentially a collection of modest second homes, attractively and compactly arranged according to a plan and "urban" and "architectural" codes that were initially conceived to bind together and exact a modicum of civility from houses that the planners and developer expected "were either going to come out of magazines or be done on the kitchen table or by plan services."[23] But in fact, the architectural definition of Seaside, which forms much of the basis of its popular appeal, has been elicited not simply through the quasi-bureaucratic indirection of the codes, but through the active and unanticipated participation of a number of young architects and designers emanating chiefly from New Haven. Unlike the Woods at Bath or Richard Norman Shaw at Bedford Park, Duany and Plater-Zyberk have purposely refrained from building at Seaside themselves, in order to concentrate on its planning and the matter of inducing an "authentic" architectural variety, that they felt to be beyond the means of a single firm.[24] The codes are promulgated by Davis as developer, advised by Duany and Plater-Zyberk, in the absence of any countervailing policy, since Seaside, as originally platted on eighty acres, was too small to be incorporated as a town under Florida law. This arrangement is not as peculiar as it might first seem, since the substitution of property owners' associations for local home rule in deliberately unincorporated suburbs is by now a well-established feature of post–World War II development practice. Duany likens the relationship of developer to planner at Seaside to that of a duke and his minister—presumably of the exterior[25]—and provisions have already been made to perpetuate the code through the agency of the Seaside Institute, which as Davis's legatee among other things, will exercise a stewardship modeled after the operation of the Hampstead Garden Suburb Trust in England.[26] Although Duany and Plater-Zyberk point to the operation of somewhat similar and visibly effective "codes" in Williamsburg, Santa Barbara, and Coral Gables (where they themselves live), the immediate "intellectual stimulus" for the codes has been assigned to Robert A. M. Stern,[27] whose Subway Suburb project for the South Bronx, presented as part of the American exhibit at the 1976 Venice Biennale, adopted "known functional paradigms . . . reintroducing historical allusion into the design: Regency Crescents, the University of Virginia, the small-town American porch, Forest Hills Gardens . . ." and selected as a "basic housing type . . . the freestanding cottage of the American small town, circa 1900."[28]

The architectural code of Seaside is concerned mainly with technique, and specifies for its cottage "villas" an undressed, "vernacular" and southernized balloon frame version of the shingle style (which in its day was actually something of an intercoastal style, though seldom seen in the South except for occasional transplants, such as Louis Sullivan's compound at Ocean Springs). The "urban" code is a three-dimensional, typologically varied template that specifies eight types over eighty acres. It functions as a town architect in absentia—as the diagrammatic, textually minimal equivalent of Weinbrenner at Karlsruhe or Shaw at Bedford Park, interpreted by a young resident architect in consulation with the developer and, via fax and telephone, his "minister." The codes assume, in Duany's words, "the incompetence or ill-will of the designer,"[29] and so anticipate a series of worst case scenarios that might threaten the formal peaceableness and intimacy of what is essentially a pre-Downing, pre-Olmsted vision of a suburb, cast not in the image of the countryside, but in that of a small town with no real place for buildings to hide.

If, in theory, architecture at Seaside is not to be depended on and may even be suspect in a postheroic, post-1950s Sarasota mode of apprehension; and if, in practice, the small house that makes up most of the (east) half of Seaside that has

110
Drexel Turner

been built to date is inherently beneath the attention of most mature architects (even when mature budgets are involved), then Seaside, as a half, has been generally well served by the aptitude of its mostly youthful practitioners and the bureaucratic ministration of the codes. Apart from the much publicized, well-carpentered cute of Krier's (twice used?) house for himself, much of the rest of Seaside comprises self-effacing and occasionally quite poised efforts, such as those by Deborah Berke (the Yearling-esque, screen-porched Hodges House); Robert Orr and Melanie Taylor (the stripped Victorian Rosewalk court, the most picturesque and widely imitated—and tacitly condescended to—of all projects within Seaside); and John Massengale (the Dawson House, a post-Jeffersonian Pavilion "built in a classical language . . . not intended for private buildings at Seaside," according to the monograph). None, however, invites canonical comparison with Venturi and Rauch's small companion pieces on Nantucket (Trubek and Wislocki, 1972) and Block Island (Cox-Hayden, 1981) upheld by Scully in his postscript to *American Architecture and Urbanism*,[30] or Moore and Turnbull's adroit California timberline excursions of the 1960s and 1970s, although Berke's Hodges House affects the screened-porch veiled simplicity of the Budge House (Healdsburg, 1966) to advantage.

Despite the codes, isolated and intrusive domestic instances of neomodernist brinksmanship have volunteered, as Neil Levine notes, posing as "strong and tough statements [to be] read by eager critics as 'reassuring evidence that the town's soundly drafted design rules need not promote an excess of cuteness or mandate historicism.'"[31] These can also be interpreted, in Plater-Zyberk's words, as evidence of the difficulty some architects have in coming "to terms with themselves for designing in a vernacular mode for Southerners in a resort, when their work is supposed to be offering some sort of polemic to northeastern architects."[32] In this respect, it is possible to group Berke and McWhorter's Schmidt House; Victoria Casasco's Appell House; and Walter Chatham's twin-dachshund house for himself and his three recent "rowhouses." For the record, these aberrations are cited by Duany and Plater-Zyberk as evidence of a benign latitudinarianism latent in the code. But they might be viewed also as an argument for the amateurism that the codes deliberately sought to enable (as a diagrammatic simplification of Christopher Alexander's pattern language)[33] and which Vitruvius advocates on occasion as a matter of self-defense: "When I see that this grand art is boldly professed by the uneducated and the unskillful, and by men who, far from being acquainted with architecture, have no knowledge even of the carpenter's trade, I can find nothing but praise for those householders who, in the confidence of learning, are emboldened to build for themselves. Their judgement is that, if they must trust to inexperienced persons, it is more becoming to them to use up a good round sum at their own pleasure than at that of a stranger."[34] For corroboration, the monograph illustrates a group of self-designed houses that are said, like Davis's designs for his own house and Seaside's post office, to have achieved "an appropriate austerity that has eluded some trained designers."[35]

Fig. 8.5. Steven Holl, Dreamland Heights, Seaside, Florida, 1984–88. Photo: Steven Brooke.

Fig. 8.6. Leon Krier, Krier/Wolff House, Seaside, Florida, 1983–88. Photo: Steven Brooke.

The brooding, domesticated Rossiana of Steven Holl's Dreamland Heights, completed in 1989, forms what is presently Seaside's most prominent public building, succeeding Davis's ultradiminutive roadside post office in the capacity. The post office continues for now to occupy the site just inside the common that will eventually receive Krier's tower, and represents the sort of useful folly occasionally found in the South, like the tiny temple/plantation office behind the main house at Eutaw, South Carolina (ca. 1810). Holl's insula exhibits no similarly discernible affiliation with the region at hand and seems outwardly more attuned to the early twentieth-century beachside manner of Irving Gill and Rudolph Schindler in southern California. It *is,* however, diagrammatically resourceful as an "urban" armature, employing a habitable, thickened-"billdingboard" section to face the common with a four-story front, making the most out of a limited program in a glorified Dodge-City way. It forms the first increment of what according to code will be a series of party-wall buildings having commercial ground floors with apartments and lodgings above surrounding the common, which will be served by a continuous, "large" (two-stories in practice) arcade broken only at street crossings. The fronts of the buildings are to vary in height (up to a maximum of five stories) in emulation of small-town main streets. But despite its schematic cleverness (enhanced by picturesquely canopied maisonettes that rise, chimney-like, behind the live-in streetfront), the assertive neomodernism of Dreamland Heights lacks the ensemble felicity to engage the *rest* of Seaside in a neighborly way, and seems in the end calculated to make the town "a community of strangers" (Holl's characterization of the building itself).[36]

The appreciable dose of "attitude" in Dreamland Heights underscores, in company with the handful of similarly inapposite houses, Scully's fear that Seaside's authors "might be giving way before the pressure of the architectural community to do all the wrong things despite themselves," subverting, as it were, the object which is "not conformity but decent behavior and intelligent conversation" and that "whatever their ingrained bias for freedom, they cannot leave the kind of loophole into which trendy posturing can insert itself to the detriment of the environment as a whole."[37] Levine makes the same point, asking "how soon a bit of stretching of the code here or pushing of it there, in the name of neo-modernism, will result in the erosion of the very structure of the town the urban code is supposed to be able, in the abstract, to maintain."[38]

Despite Duany's personal enthusiasm for Rossi's typologically reductive and repetitive urbanism, played out against the harder, more resonant streetscapes of Milan and Turin,[39] the mating of Dreamland Heights and Seaside still seems puzzling in view of Duany's espousal of pictorially cohesive values for the fulfillment of Seaside. Ostensibly, Duany's aspirations for Seaside would seem to favor Krier's vision of the city as an orderly house in which residential and commercial buildings can be designed almost anonymously "according to a very simple set of rules, of heights, of use, of different styles and proportions," and where public buildings would be provided by a "few architects" of select ability whose "work is predictable" and congenially so.[40] Krier's own small house and fragmentary hints of a *res publica* for Seaside suggest a more empathetic if formulaic civic mode, essayed as a revernacularization of the classical like that predicted by Alan Colquhoun, in which "we are likely to find traces of those elements of high style which originally belonged to a sophisticated and highly developed architecture of monuments—the very antithesis of vernacular building."[41] The scenographic, neo-Claudian aspect of Krier's oeuvre, noted by Scully as well as Colin Rowe,[42] has even prompted Rowe to wonder (pace Scully and the reapplication of the stick and shingle styles) whether "if we can approach the irregularities of the Hadrianic picturesque (with *exactly* the same details) then why not try?"[43]

Duany is not yet prepared to take such a leap, although he still maintains that at least in visual terms "to make a town harmonious . . . requires a narrowing of the architectural possibilities. Any town that is good looking enough to appear on a travel poster has a limited range of architectural elements. Charleston is one of these . . . Nantucket another . . . and Seaside has that ambition . . . and in the end it will be a poster-quality town. . . . We are willing to loosen it up if we must . . . but we are equally interested in tightening up. We are very intrigued by eighteenth century urbanism: street after street of completely steady cornice lines, and very slight variation."[44] Emily Post, inveighing in 1930 against "a species for whom there is no better name than neighborhood destroyers," citing the arrival of an unwanted architectural guest on an "old South Carolina street," neatly anticipates Duany's sensibility and fan-shaped window of opportunity: If each of us in every town would care something about the unity of the streets we live on, the towns of America would be the most beautiful in the world. . . . Perhaps the only way to create a town of beautiful accord would be to start with a brand-new development and lay out its streets with restrictions of each."[45]

So far, Seaside's poster qualities derive almost exclusively from strategic pockets of well-appointed cottages, with their code-mandated porches; lot-defining, three-foot-high white picket fences (Olmsted prescribed fences for Riverside; Levitt forbade them); well-mannered fenestration (no picture windows allowed); coordinated exterior colors (no houses in white, excepting Krier's, a prohibition enforced by Downing too); soffit free under eaves and sufficiently pitched roofs; meticulously screened air-conditioning compressors and precision-placed "mushroom" pathlights. Slender towers (a Sullivanian accoutrement at Ocean Springs) are purposely encouraged, in Duany's words "so that even the most landlocked has a shot at the ocean view" and also in anticipation that "the towers . . . will be very significant to the image of Seaside; Seaside is going to be a city of towers, unlike any I know of in America."[46] Outbuildings and detached garages (the only kind permitted) dot and cross the figure ground. Side yards are mandated where applicable; streets are deliberately shrunken as are front yards (in the manner observed by Moore in Charleston and on Davis Street in Edgartown[47] in contrast to

Drexel Turner

Olmsted's deep setbacks at Riverside).[48] The polygonal (rather than curved, to simplify the construction of fences, according to Duany)[49] fanning of the town plan about the common also serves to promote picturesque jumbles. Even the parking provisions of the "urban" code abet a kind of valet-parking showmanship by explicitly exempting "air-stream type" trailers from the otherwise uniform requirement that "trucks, boats, campers and trailers . . . shall be parked in rear yards only."[50]

Perhaps the most unobtrusively gratifying aspect of the dressing of Seaside is the landscaping initiated by Andres Duany's brother, Douglas, during the first years of development as a noticeably shaggy, crazy-salad counterpoint to Seaside's otherwise pristine mien. This preservation and nurturing of local plant materials of seldom acknowledged dignity recalls Sullivan's appreciation of the native landscape at Ocean Springs, with its pines of all kinds and "patriarchal sweet gums and black gums with their younger broods; maples, hickories, myrtles; in the undergrowth, dogwoods, halesias, sloe plums, buckeyes and azaleas, all in a riot of bloom . . . all grouped and arranged as though by the hand of an unseen poet."[51] The effect of Seaside's regionally attentive landscaping, furrowed by white picket fences, may someday be barely distinguishable from that of coastal villages like Summerville, South Carolina, begun a century and a half ago with a similar solicitude for vegetation.

The reality of Seaside today lies somewhere between the "sweet disorder" that prevailed among five hundred cottages on thirty-four acres at Wesleyan Grove[52] (though transposed, somewhat plainer and unfretted, at a late-twentieth-century, second-house scale that makes room for cars as well as Airstream trailers and their poor relations) and the less nostalgic, pretime-share, auto-nomadic Americana of the decentralized motel and garden apartment resort (though realized more decorously and on a more shapely plan). At the confirmed reservations end of the spectrum, the *Seaside Times* refer to the town's Cottage Rental Agency as the "hub of Seaside" ("more than 6,000 room nights" booked for 1992 before the year began), while *House Beautiful*'s correspondent adverts to "housekeeping carts [that] whir by carrying soap and towels" on streets whose cars "have license plates from as far away as Illinois" in a town where "only 12 families live year-round."[53]

In a similar vein, Duany and Plater-Zyberk sought unsuccessfully in 1985 to extend the post-Albertian notion of "motel as small city/city as large motel" with the design of a 3,250-bedroom, detached motel for Walt Disney World in Orlando, along lines suggested by the plan of Savannah.[54]

Duany at times complains that at Seaside "we're constantly fighting off the Disney syndrome," but the scenographic units, though miniaturized and colorized in a manner not unlike Disney's (Plater-Zyberk has compared the houses to "toys"), seem more apt to from its somewhat bloodless, comparatively upscale variant, Ralph-Lauren-slept-here syndrome.[55] Aspects of Seaside are even now being assimilated by Disney itself to add to Orlando's ever-expanding menu of themed delights, most particularly Disney's first time-share venture. This venture casts a more-than-passing glance at Seaside in its effort to simulate "the romance of turn-of-the-century Key West" complete with man-made "white sand beach" and specially equipped "one-, two-, and three-bedroom, pastel-colored, luxurious vacation homes offering microwave, refrigerator, stove, convenience store, VCR and indoor whirlpool tub."[56]

As Charles Moore advised on taking leave of Edgartown, "Perfunctory attempts to 'fit' tastefully risk being lifeless, since care . . . has to be felt personally and delivered personally and cannot yet be simulated in the catalogue or in the lumber yard"[57]—a reality that confronts Seaside no less than the time-share margins of Disney World, code or no code. Duany's own predilection for Seaside's "look" is closer to that of Hitchcock's Rhode Island mill villages and the "'relatively ascetic' aesthetic"[58] of his and Plater-Zyberk's architectural work, which is to say sparer than most of what has been built, as though waiting for Tessenow to show up in pine siding, painted in shades more uniform and severe than the prevailing Seaside palette, the varied cheeriness of which Duany views as working "against a harmonious urbanism" even though it helps "the marketing quite a lot . . . eighties Americans like pretty things."[59] Much of what has been built Duany regards with neo-Veblenian discomfort, as the imprint of a "public that has been conditioned to expect . . . a very high degree of cute, they have no taste whatsoever for 'quiet simplicity or majestic grandeur' but prefer pretty, perky, happy architecture. We personally find sweet buildings difficult to provide because we don't sympathize with the self-indulgent society that loves them so. Seaside is by no means free of that, and it should be made clear that the code does not enforce cute buildings . . . but it does allow the owners to exercise their preference for them. Somebody once said . . . that we had designed Kansas, but were building Oz."[60]

Whether or not Kansas belongs in Florida, what Seaside lacks at the moment is any very demonstrable civic and social core. For the time being, the civic collation of Seaside is suggested simply by the unstaked outline of its plan on the ground, the core of which is tangential, if not superfluous, to the thicket of cottages built up on its east end. The only plastic notion of the development that may one day form an appreciable ring around the common issues abruptly from Holl's Dreamland Heights, to which has been appended a lumpish market and meeting hall by Deborah Berke at the point where the plan begins to crank. The code-specified perimeter arcade for the common might provide the basis for a sufficiently encompassing, promissory gesture in three dimensions if fully realized in advance of the buildings themselves—a custom-built ruin like that suggested by the virtually detached, proto-nostalgic disposition of Paul Rudolph's John Wal-

116
Drexel Turner

lace House (Athens, Alabama, 1961–64), or the lighter, tacked-on, three-story arcade that once stretched 450 feet across the Broadway front of the Grand Union Hotel in Saratoga Springs. One wonders why no buildable, comprehensive treatment for this element was not settled on from the outset, if not actually begun in the prefatory manner of the Place Vendôme or Coral Gables' picturesquely wrought Puerta del Sol, as a bare-bones exedra for Krier's transformational pharos. Although another building fronting on the common may soon be realized across from Holl's by Machado and Silvetti (incorporating a program identical to that of Dreamland Heights), its additive effect is inherently limited, confronted with the unmediated gap between the two.

Meanwhile, the non-polity of Seaside has come to frequent a beachfront restaurant, Bud and Alley's Oyster Bar, that has grown Topsylike from two slight cottages. While Bud and Alley's has proved a semipiquant boon to community life (and also constitutes Seaside's most prominent adaptive reuse project), its precise placement, Duany observes, is also a matter of "lousy urbanism," since it will obstruct the axial connection of Krier's tower to the water."[61] Still, the modest success of this unexceptional, improvisationally located eatery would seem to suggest the potential for something approaching the neighborhood "casinos" (actually zero-lot-line-country-clubs) realized by McKim, Mead and White for the seasonal populations of Newport, Narragansett Pier, and Short Hills. As a basis for resort sodality, such a well-bred pleasure pier of neo-WASP pretension might entice at least part of the "society of strangers" from homebound suppers of gourmet take-out harvested from Seaside's Modica Market (which, at Davis's behest, stocks "only a handful of bottled salad dressings" but "dozens of bottles of virgin olive oils" and vinegars)[62] and the self-sufficient sociability of cable television, Nintendo, video players and hot tub grottoes (screened, one supposes, according to code).

But since even twenty-six vinegar solutions may not be enough, the impresario of Seaside is contemplating attractions of a tonier sort, to be presented under the auspices of the multivalent, Chautauquaesque, Seaside Institute. According to Davis, the institute is intended to evolve from its present pattern of occasional lectures and related presentations to something "world-class" based on the experiences of "Malboro or Tanglewood or Aspen,"[63] though the matter of where the cars would be parked, once the just-planned, more than fivefold expansion of Seaside's initial eighty acres comprising three new neighborhoods[64] is fully subscribed, is not entirely clear. Not that this *deus ex cultura* is ordinarily available to most eighty-acre subdivisons, but the town hall/conference center lot has already been redesignated "lyceum" and the common as "amphitheater" on the map of Seaside and one hesitates to discount Davis's ability to market this vision as a means of "helping Seaside become more vital than it is, if not necessarily messier."[65]

After slightly more than a decade of development that began in 1981, Seaside has achieved an astonishing celebrity and has, unlike most towns, even deemed it prudent to seek trademark protection in its own name. The still very partial results have already been valorized by HRH the Prince of Wales sight unseen in his informal tract, *A Vision of Britain,* presumably on Krier's say-so.[66] Seaside appears as the most extensively illustrated project in Vincent Scully's 1967–88 postscript to *American Architecture and Urbanism,* and Robert A. M. Stern accords it as much attention as Llewelyn Park and Riverside in his well charted PBS television series companion piece, *Pride of Place.*[67] The Harvard Graduate School of Design's exhibition and catalogue of 1991, surveying the "town-making" activities of Duany and Plater-Zyberk, assigns epochal importance to Davis's eighty acres with an introductory essay titled "Since (and Before) Seaside";[68] it also serves as an honorific updating of the Architectural League of New York's just post–ground-breaking Seaside exhibition of 1985, from which sprang Mohney and Easterling's helpfully detailed monograph. In 1990 the American Academy in Rome, simultaneously and perspicaciously, awarded fellowships to both Seaside's developer, Robert Davis, and its photographer of record, Steven Brooke, whose particular contribution to the public (and critical reception of Seaside's "news from nowhere") Levine also affirms.[69]

Fifty years ago, E. B. White professed to "love Florida . . . for the remains of her unfinished cities . . . [where] dead sidewalks run off into the live jungle . . . cabbage palms throw their spiny shade across the stillborn streets . . . creepers bind old curbstones in a fierce sensual embrace and the mockingbirds dwell in song upon the remembered grandeur of real estate's purple hour."[70] But although Seaside by now seems likely to evade the romantic possibilities of premature ruination, whether it can actually live up to its prodigious notices whether it can actually live up to its prodigious notices and become more than just another avatar of sophisticated press relations and downsized leisure-class pursuits has yet to be established. Seaside may even be hampered in this respect by false starts and a disdain for some of the very things that contribute, unpretentiously and without thought to architectural posturing, to its fundamentally self-varnishing appeal. Resort architecture and "urbanism," whether on the Bath or Brighton models, have always held the potential to be translated to real life for pleasure and profit. Perhaps as Seaside develops, the lessons to be learned from it will prove to be more, not less, than meet the eye, though the means to assure such a result may be both simpler and more tenuous than its authors realize. As John Ruskin, for whom, presumably not without reflection, a principal street in Seaside is named, observed: "It is no sign of deadness in a present art that it borrows or imitates, but only if it borrows without paying interest, or if it imitates without choice."[71]

Notes

1. Keller Easterling, "Public Enterprise" (revised from the *Princeton Architectural* *Journal* 2 (Princeton, N.J.: Princeton Architectural Press, 1985) 35–43) in David

Mohney and Keller Easterling, eds., *Seaside: Making a Town in America* (New York: Princeton Architectural Press, 1991), 48–60.

2. The phrase "suburban sadness" is David Riesman's. Jefferson describes the private buildings of Virginia settlements as "ugly, uncomfortable, and happily . . . perishable" and the houses as built on but "two or three plans" in his *Notes on the State of Virginia* (1785); reprinted in Merrill Peterson, ed., *The Portable Thomas Jefferson* (New York: Viking Penguin, 1975), 202.

3. Easterling, "Public Enterprise," 56.

4. Louis Sullivan, *The Autobiography of an Idea* (American Institute of Architects, 1924; reprint ed., New York: Dover, 1956), 295.

5. Sam Shepard, *The Curse of the Starving Class* (1976–78) in *Sam Shepard: Seven Plays* (New York: Bantam, 1981), 163.

6. Alexis de Tocqueville, *Democracy in America,* vol. 2 (1835, Henry Reeve, tr.; reprint ed., New York: Knopf, 1945), 54.

7. Easterling, "Public Enterprise," 56.

8. Spiro Kostof, *The City Shaped: Urban Patterns and Meanings Through History* (Boston: Bulfinch, 1991), 277.

9. (Marcus) Vitruvius Pollio, *The Ten Books on Architecture* (1914, Morris Morgan, tr.; reprint ed., New York, 1960), 31.

10. Georg Simmel, "Fashion," 1904, collected in Donald N. Levine, ed., *Georg Simmel: On Individuality and Social Forms* (Chicago: Univ. of Chicago Press, 1971), 305.

11. Henry-Russell Hitchcock, Jr., *Rhode Island Architecture* (Providence: Rhode Island Museum Press, 1939), 36, 40.

12. "Delightsome (as their builders would have said)" is offered in appreciation of Ellen Weiss's *City in the Woods: The Life and Design of an American Camp Meeting on Martha's Vineyard* (New York: Oxford Univ. Press, 1987). Moore appends his description of the plan of Oak Bluffs to an account of Edgartown in Charles Moore, Gerald Allen, and William Turnbull, *The Place of Houses* (New York: Holt, Rinehart, and Winston, 1974), 18.

13. Moore, "Edgartown," in *The Place of Houses,* 14.

14. Ibid., 18.

15. Vincent Scully, Jr., "Seaside and New Haven," in Alex Krieger with William Lennertz, eds., *Andres Duany and Elizabeth Plater-Zyberk: Towns and Town-Making Principles* (New York: Harvard Graduate School of Design/Rizzoli, 1991), 17, 18.

16. Ibid., 18, 19.

17. Ibid., 19.

18. David Mohney, "Interview with Andres Duany," 1986, in Mohney and Easterling, *Seaside,* 62. Hereafter cited as Duany interview.

19. Ibid., 62.

20. "The House of Leon Krier at Seaside," *Composicion Arquitectonica* June, 1989, 40.

21. *The Charlottesville Tapes: Transcript of the Conference at the University of Virginia School of Architecture, 12–13 November 1982* (New York: Rizzoli, 1985), 22.

22. Neil Levine, "Questioning the View: Seaside's Critique of the Gaze of Modern Architecture," in Mohney and Easterling, *Seaside,* 254.

23. David Mohney, "Interview with Elizabeth Plater-Zyberk," 1989, in Mohney and Easterling, *Seaside,* 77. Hereafter cited as Plater-Zyberk interview.

24. Duany interview, 63.

25. Ibid., 70.

26. "The Seaside Institute," information sheet, undated.

27. Janet Abrams, "The Form of the (American) City: Two Projects by Andres Duany and Elizabeth Plater-Zyberk," *Lotus* 50 (1986), 10.

28. Robert A. M. Stern, "Subway Suburb," *The Anglo-American Suburb, Architectural Design Profile,* 1981, 92.

29. Duany interview, 73.

30. Vincent Scully, Jr., *American Architecture and Urbanism* (1969; revised ed., New York: Henry Holt, 1988, 257–59.

31. Levine, "Questioning the View," 241.

32. Plater-Zyberk interview, 78.

33. Duany interview, 64–65.

34. Vitruvius, *The Ten Books,* 169.

35. Moheny and Easterling, *Seaside,* 232.

36. Steven Holl, *Anchoring: Selected Projects, 1975–88* (New York: Princeton Architectural Press, 19   ), 81.

37. Scully, "Seaside and New Haven," 19–20.

38. Levine, "Questioning the View," 255.

39. Duany interview, 70.

40. *Charlottesville Tapes,* 23.

41. Alan Colquhoun, "Vernacular Classicism," *Architectural Design* 54:5/6 (1984), 29.

42. Scully, *American Architecture and Urbanism,* 265. Colin Rowe, "The Revolt of the Senses," *Architectural Design* 54:7/8 (1984), 8, refers to Krier's" . . . William Morris world . . . contrived out of Ledoux/Schinkel bits and pieces, with a dash of Poussin and a large tribute to Claude. . ."

43. Rowe, "Revolt of the Senses," 18.

44. Duany interview, 70.

45. Emily Post, *The Personality of a House* (New York: Funk and Wagnalls, 1930), 54–56.

46. Duany interview, 66.

47. Charles Moore, "Southernness," *Perspecta* 15 (1975), 12.

48. In a prescriptive conclusion, the authors of *The Place of Houses* reflect on the "prevalent tyrannies" of "vast, minimum-standard roads . . . (and) space that is abandoned to setbacks . . . in (a) suburbia of abstractly derived and slavishly maintained lawns," 271.

49. Duany interview, 62.

50. "Urban Code—The Town of Seaside," in Moheny and Easterling, *Seaside,* 98–99.

51. Sullivan, *The Autobiography of an Idea,* 297.

52. Ellen Weiss, *City in the Woods,* 37.

53. "Cottage Rental Agency is Hub of Seaside," *The Seaside Times,* Winter, 1992, 4; Jane Margolies, "Halfway to Paradise," *House Beautiful,* Apr., 1992, 107.

54. Abrams, *Two Projects by Andres Duany and Elizabeth Plater-Zyberk,* 11–12, 14–15.

55. Ibid., 11.

56. Michael J. Crosbie, "Vacation Club, Walt Disney World, Orlando Florida," *Architec-ture* May, 1992, 51; advertisement, *New York Times Magazine* Mar. 17, 1992, 2:5. The residential units were designed by Bassenian/Lagoni of Santa Ana Heights, California, and the "Club House" by Richardson Nagy.

57. Moore, *The Place of Houses,* p. 18.

58. Abrams, *Two Projects,* 12.

59. Duany interview, 72.

60. Ibid., 71.

61. Ibid., 72.

62. Beth Dunlop, "Coming of Age," *Architectural Record,* July, 1989, 98, 100; Margolies, "Halfway to Paradise," 117. According to Dunlop, Seaside's vacationers are disposed to "buy less" at the Modica Market "so they can return often" to what she calls "the pivotal element in the town's maturation."

63. "Robert Davis Returns From Italy," *The Seaside Times,* Fall, 1991, 1.

64. Moheny and Easterling, *Seaside,* 106–107.

65. "Seaside Awarded an A," *The Seaside Times,* Winter, 1992, 1.

66. HRH The Prince of Wales, *A Vision of Britain: A Personal View of Architecture* (New York: Doubleday, 1989), 142–46. Krier functions as an advisor to the prince, who salutes Davis as having "challenged most of the urban design thinking of the time and made a commercial success of building to the highest standards," but also observes that: "The founders certainly believe that a sense of real community will grow here; that people will live here. I wish them well. But—even with the sensible regulations—a sense of community is not easily achieved."

67. Robert A. M. Stern, *Pride of Place: Building the American Dream* (Boston: Houghton Mifflin, 1986), 166–67.

68. Alex Krieger, in Krieger and Lennertz, *Andres Duany and Elizabeth Plater-Zyberk,* 9–16.

69. Levine, "Questioning the View," 241.

70. E. B. White, "On a Florida Key," *Harper's,* Feb., 1941.

71. John Ruskin, *The Seven Lamps of Architecture* (1848; reprint ed., New York: Noonday Press, 1974), 145.

Edge of a City

Stephen Holl

9

On the fringe of the modern city, displaced fragments sprout without intrinsic relationships to existing organization, other than that of the camber and loops of the curvilinear freeway. The exploration of strategies to counter sprawl at the periphery of cities—the formation of spaces rather than the formation of objects—are primary aims of our Edge of a City projects. In each proposal, living, working, recreational, and cultural facilities are juxtaposed in new pedestrian sectors that might act as social condensers for new communities. From "spatial retaining bars" that protect the desert at the edge of Phoenix, Arizona, to void courts that internalize the landscape in Fukoka, Japan, the six plans attempt an entwining with existing circumstances. Though they differ in form, these proposals share a "pretheoretical ground" of psychological space, program, movement, light quality, and tactility.

The edge of a city is a philosophical region, where city and natural landscape overlap, existing without choice or expectation. Here the "thrown away" spreads itself outward like nodal lines of a stone tossed into a pond. This zone calls for visions and projections to delineate the boundary between the urban and the rural. Visions of a city's future can be plotted on this partially spoiled land, liberating the remaining natural landscape, protecting the habitat of the hundreds of species of animals and plants that are threatened with extinction. Traditional planning methods are no longer adequate. Looking back at the city from the point of view of the landscape, these projects consider untested programs and new kinds of urban spaces.

The exponential changes brought about by air travel over this century exemplify how experiences of space and time change from city to city. Within hours we are transported from one climate and time zone into another. Formerly, entering a city occurred along the earth via a bridge or a portal. Today we circle over then jet down to an airstrip on a city's periphery. Consequently, in making plans and projections for new city edges, it is necessary to discard old methods and working habits and begin with basic research.

Fig. 9.1 Fukuoka void space/hinged space housing.

Fig. 9.2. Fukuoka void space/hinged space housing.

Psychological Space

Psychological space is at the core of spatial experience. It is intertwined with the subjective impression of actual spatial geometry and born in the imagination. The absolute side of rational planning is in a contrapuntal relationship to the pathological nature of the human soul. It is in this mix, at its architectonic conception, that the spatial spirit of a work of architecture is determined.

Sitting in a fishing boat, drifting a few miles away from the ocean shore, one is surrounded by horizon. Reflections of clouds in the water double the space of the sky; the ocean provokes a silent, inward-focusing mood, psychological as well as spatial. Likewise, the experience of flight, with its views of space between cloud formations, has a vastness of dimension that invigorates and excites the imagination. Towers of white clouds bunch independently like cotton skyscrapers. Looking down, the desert floor below seems to be a base for these strange forms, then

122

suddenly, jet wings cut the towers in half and the mobile architecture of the clouds is sliced by immense aluminum knives. The spatial exhilaration of air travel has transformed humanity, and the vaporous architecture of the clouds has become a phenomenal spatial experience. The psychic core of a room is like reverie. The room, an individual's place of periodic repose, either inspires or inhibits creative thought. Insight, fantasies, and imagination are fueled by the psychological space of the private interior.

If we consider the interior as the harbor of the soul, light, colors, textures, and spatial relationships take on an absolute and urgent importance. The interior, a "psychic vessel of containment," can possess both the clarity and vagueness required for reflection, fantasy, and passion. The architecture of the interior can alter our experience of the time of day or season; it can alter our perception of colors, affecting our mood and body temperature. At this direct encounter with interior space, architecture changes the way we live.

Just as the dimension of the soul is depth (not breadth) so the dimensions of an interior may well exist below or above the physical limits of its geometry. Spatial extensions beyond a room's interior, those in a room flanking an open court, for example, may engage and extend the spirit of that interior. Thus spatial projection can be a way of invigorating minimal spaces in housing or in places of confinement, such as hospital rooms. Concepts of "void space" and "hinged space" extend the spatial sense of the living areas in twenty-eight apartments in a housing scheme for Fukuoka, Japan. Four open courts bracket natural ponds on the south, and four open gravel courts face an enclosed park space on the north, extending the interiors and offering a variety of perspectival experiences. On the interiors, "hinged space" formed by pivoting "participating" walls transforms a four-bedroom plan into a free plan, allowing spatial adjustments according to cycles of growth and decline in family size or changing activities of daily life.

Passage/Parallax
In the yet-to-be-built city, notions of passage through the city must be addressed. Consider the city as it might appear in a series of cinematic images: zoom shots in front of a person walking, tracking shots along the side, the view changing as the head turns. At the same time, the city is a place to be felt. Notions of space, shifting ground, plan, section, and expansion are bound up in passage through the city. Consider movement through the city framed by vertical buildings. Each change of position reframes a new spatial field. This parallax of overlapping fields changes with the angles of the sun and with the glow of the sky. Premonitions of unknown means of communication and passage suggest a variety of new urban spaces.

In the modern city the voids between buildings, not the buildings themselves, hold spatial inspiration. Urban space is formed by vertical groupings, terrestrial shifts, elongated slots of light, bridges, and vertical penetrations of a fixed horizontal. Urban space has a vertical Z dimension equal to or more important than the horizontal X-Y plane. This perpendicular spatial order is amplified by a range of viewpoints from various levels. From a roof terrace, a subway platform, the upper floors of a tower, or an underpass, urban perspective in the Z dimension is experienced on a shifting ground plane.

The experience of parallax, the change in the arrangement of surfaces defining space due to the changing position of the viewer, is transformed into oblique planes of movement. Spatial definition is ordered by angles of perception.

In the 1990 proposal for parallax skyscrapers to be built on the Hudson River in Manhattan, ultrathin towers bracket views and form a new kind of framed urban space over water. The existing railyard would be transformed into a new city edge park, in the spirit of Frederick Law Olmsted. Hybrid buildings with diverse functions, the towers are linked by a horizontal underwater transit system that connects to high speed elevators serving upper transfer lobbies.

Program/Activity

The incredible energy in such cities as New York, Milan, and Paris is related to programmatic diversity and juxtaposition. Modern metropolitan life is characterized by fluctuating activities, turbulent shifts in demographics, and changing desires of restless populations.

We do not call for a new disordered architecture to match the disorder of culture; such duplication simply affirms the chaotic, achieving no other dimension. Rather, we propose experiments in search of new orders, the projection of new relationships. This is not to transpose our study into a system or method, and yet the energy inherent in the development of new relationships presents us with a continuity of ordering that inspires reflection.

Consider the experience of reading a comprehensive morning newspaper, an ordering of life in society. The following untenable juxtapositions might be paralleled in urban terms: an article describing a billion-ton floating glacier that is drifting around the North Pole lies next to an article about the construction of a twenty-four-foot-diameter water tunnel and a piece on the austerity program of a religious cult; alongside a column on insomnia and the sleep movement of plants is a huge diagram of the Pacific Rim trade network; an article on Japanese factories in Mexico is adjacent to a photograph of a hole in the ozone layer over the South Pole.

To translate precisely thoughts and feelings sparked by such relationships is as problematic as translating an English word into all of the world's 2,796 languages. Precision of the rational gives way to intuition; subjective dimensions establish physical dimensions.

Fig. 9.3. Dallas–Fort Worth Spiroid Sector Institute of Science Sec. (left), Maglev Sec. (right).

A spatial arrangement, an aroma, a musical phrase, may be imagined simultaneously. Depending on the awareness and imagination of the perceiver, an initial visual field can provoke subject matter and imply programs. We can speak of the sounds implied by an array of brittle linear forms, or the way a view smells. An individual's cultural associations, recognition of materials, and imagination of their properties, and the physiological effects of space and enclosure all present individual limitations. The perceiver's angle of vision and preconception is potentially open to unforeseen associations. Rather than allowing prejudice to be a

Fig. 9.4. Cleveland dam model.

126
Stephen Holl

primary subjective determinant, one can induce program associations by increasing the possible number of programs to occupy an urban setting.

Isolated buildings of a single function, the suburban norm, typical at the modern city's periphery, give way in these projects to hybrid buildings with diverse programs. An effort toward programmatic richness—an open association of spaces to program suggestions (action images)—is fertilized by gathering and juxtaposing a variety of activities.

In a 1986 project for the reuse of the Porta Vittoria railyard in Milan, free association, "semiautomatic" programming is a strategy for increasing diversity and juxtaposition. From a dense center, Milan unfolds in circles ringed by a patchwork grid that finally sprawls raggedly into the landscape. Against this centrifugal urban sprawl (from dense core to light periphery), a reversal is proposed: light and fine-grained toward the center, heavy and volumetric toward the periphery. This proposal projects a new ring of density and intensity adjoining the rolling green of a reconstituted landscape. A new strategy for urban morphology is explored; perspective of overlapping imagined urban spaces are drawn and projected backward into plan fragments. With the help of a sectional "correlational chart" these space fragments are adjusted to form a whole city sector.

A very different strategy is proposed in the "stitch plan" for Cleveland, 1989. Five "Xs" spaced along the inland periphery of Cleveland define precise crossover points from a new urban area to a clarified rural region. These new urban sectors are made up of spaces bounded by buildings with a mixture of functions. At one "X" the crossover is developed into a dam with hybrid functions. The urban section includes a hotel, a cinema, and a gymnasium. The rural section contains programs related to nature: a fish hatchery, an aquarium, botanical gardens. The artificial lake formed by the dam provides a large recreational area and extends the crossover point into a boundary line. Taken together, the "Xs" imply an urban edge.

The "Edge of a City" projects probe phenomenological dimensions in the formation of new urban spaces, in order to transform the tangled waste at the fringes of our modern cities and to build new urban sectors with programmatic spatial and architectural richness. Beyond this horizon we are seeking a moving territory between the extremes of idea and physical experience. In the same way that the French philosopher Maurice suggested that the "absolute separation of meaning from factual existence in every region of experience is in fact impossible," any constructed space can be defined by its first inhabitant—a psychological space, whether of angst or joy.

10

Engaging the Highway
Bruce Webb with Martin Price

The synthetic landscape formed by a vast network of concrete freeways is a power-ful symbol of late twentieth-century urbanization. Through manifolding of their own relentless logic and engineered economies, freeways redefine the form and experience of the modern city. They draw dynamic lines which run along like precise incisions in the older fabric of cities, dismantling old organizations and creating new ones over which they frequently dominate. Once free of the com-pact grid they unravel into free-flowing streams, crossing the natural landscape and gathering to their implacable right-of-way the inchoate fragments of subur-ban settlements.

Travelers on a high speed highway encounter a rapidly unfolding sequence of ex-periences—phenomena more akin to the sequences in a motion picture than to the still pictures architects and urban designers use in their work. Considered as a point of view, motion has had a significant impact on the evolution of modern thought. In 1965, in his seminal book on *The Nature and Art of Motion,* Gyorgy Kepes described how motion has invaded the total modern experience, unbalanc-ing old concepts and setting a challenge for a "re-vision of vision":

> The inescapable attribute of our time is its runaway pace. Tidal waves of
> traffic pound us; sprawling cities and exploding populations squeeze us.
> Wildly erratic throbbing migrations—the daily shuttle from home to work,
> from work to home, the weekend surge from city to country and from coun-
> try back to city, the punctuations of rush-hour deadlocks—toss us in an ac-
> celerating rhythm barely within our control. Streams of speeding objects
> —motorcars, airplanes, intercontinental missiles, orbiting space capsules—
> weave a rapidly changing fabric all around us with patterns of spiraling
> velocities. At night, the reassuring calm of the firmament is blotted out by
> our cities, which are transformed into giant circuses where darting head-
> lights, winking traffic lights, glittering, gaudy displays, and advertising signs
> whirl and swirl and pirouette in frantic competition for our attention.[1]

In an essay titled "Science and the Deallegorization of motion,"[2] Gerald Holton describes the persistence of allegorical interpretations of motion throughout his-tory, and the subsequent deallegorization of motion phenomena through scientific and mathematical study. This understanding, however, has not spread evenly among the disciplines that study the human condition. In many instances, Kepes writes: "We have inherited concepts of order belonging to a smaller, slower scale of existence; these are becoming increasingly useless in the exploded scale of events. We have been accustomed to making ordered relationships by mapping objects and even individuals in their positions relative to one another. Now we are forced to recognize that objects do not have fixed positions . . . We have learned to recognize that a description of position tells only half the story. A still photo of a heavily trafficked street does not tell us which cars are moving and which are still. Our information must include velocity as well as position if we are to do anything about the situation."[3]

In his concluding essay in Kepes's collection, "Motion, Sequence and the City," Donald Appleyard sets forth a prospectus for the promises and potentials of this revised point of view in urban design: "As the pace of travel quickens and the cities continue to spread, motion increasingly saturates the urban experience. It is evident in the painter's brush stroke, the blurred photograph, the movie of urban life. And each day most of us, by one mode or another, travel through the city. It is not always a pleasant experience. Clutter, congestion and hazard see to that. But there are moments and there is a potential for great delight. Motion can bring a sense of freedom, vividness and power to city travel. It can enliven a dead scene. And it plays a primary role in the formulation and communication of the city image, its structure and meaning, for the city is apprehended as we move within it."[4] Coming at the end of a series of essays discussing experiments with motion in the arts, Appleyard's discussion of the highway and the city repositions the design of highways in a thematic context of kinetic art, where motion takes its place alongside the traditional design categories of form and space. But how can motion be built into the design of cities? Appleyard writes, "The environmental designer has found it easy to talk about, but difficult to manipulate. Ephemeral yet ubiquitous, it is elusive to capture, record and therefore to design."[5]

Appleyard's discussion of a method for designing with motion borrows heavily from the language and techniques of filmmaking. In a later book[6] he demonstrated how picture sequences and linear diagrams could be used by urban designers to describe and orchestrate the pattern of events unfolding along the road, in this case a portion of the Northeast Expressway in Boston.

The impact of Appleyard's methodological tools, including his later work with television monitors and large scale, detailed methods to study designs from a kinetic point of view (as well as similar work with scoring notations systems adapted from the dance by Lawrence Halprin)[7] have remained largely academic.

The design of the architecture and the spatial experiences along freeway corridors has not kept pace with the design of the roadways themselves, where a highly refined and precise technical-engineering approach has resulted in highways that satisfy a very limited range of criteria.

In many ways the design of freeways shares certain characteristics with the architecture of the early modern movement — stark, utilitarian directness; magnificent control; and functional shaping, to name a few — and, indeed, the pioneers of the modern movement embraced the problem of the highway and the automobile as a necessary extension of architecture at a variety of scales. Lawrence Halprin in his book *Freeways*[8] cites several examples of the "ultimate integration" of architecture with the design of high speed transport system including Edgar Chambliss's proposal for "Roadtown," a multilayered, linear building with a promenade on the roof, housing in the middle, and high velocity trains in the basement. Chambliss's proposal would snake through the countryside, uniting populations, services and transportation in a single, sinewy package. Similarly, Le Corbusier's 1929 scheme for an auto-linear city for Algiers placed the highway atop a curvilinear building which was itself raised on columns to preserve an uninterrupted ground plane.

But architects have, by and large, had little real impact on the design of freeways and have failed as well to develop viable, special solutions for this general class of building-context problems. Michel Foucault has commented on this diminishing role of architects in affecting the environment in which we live as a matter of professional disenfranchisement: "Architects are not the engineers or technicians of the three great variables: territory, communication and speed."[9] The consequences of this intense specialization of effort and the marginalization of the architect's role in it has resulted in great discontinuity among the elements that together create the built environment. The architecture which lines the freeway seems made up of capricious or desperate ornaments struggling to maintain a connection with the no-nonsense minimalism of the highway. The awkward spaces in between, mediated by a prosthetic architecture of signs, fail to satisfy even the most basic requirements of place making.

Lawrence Halprin cited the failure to achieve a reconciliation of the freeway with its architectural or urbanistic realm as one of failing to see the road building project itself as an artistic endeavor: "When freeways have failed, it has been because their designers have ignored their form-giving potentials and their inherent qualities as works of art in the city. They have been thought of only as traffic carriers but, in fact, they are a new form of urban sculpture for motion. To fulfill this aim freeways must be designed by people with sensitivity not only to structure but also to the environment; to the effect of freeways on the form of the city; and to the choreography of motion."[10] He continues by describing the design of a great freeway as "an intuitive act of the most demanding and imprecise kind."

Architect Martin Price's work with students in his studio at the University of

Engaging the highway with a corporate headquarters. This project explores alternatives for the development of a 3.8 million-square-foot corporate office complex presently accommodated in two forty-story towers flanking Highway 75 in downtown Dallas. The decision to limit the alternative designs to a maximum height of 120 feet was based on the height limitations of the Dallas hook-and-ladder fire trucks, as well as a desire to explore the potentials of engaging the highway with buildings that relate to the horizontal motion of the highway.

Fig. 10.1. Scheme I (Lara Ulrich Clayton and Karen Johnson) is structured by an organic network inspired by the fanning, growth pattern of tree branches. From the hard, more massive highway edge, the scheme unravels into a series of meandering pedestrian paths. The ground slopes in an inverse relationship to the building, bringing the sky below the existing ground level to create window exposures for additional office levels. This strategy also exposes the wall of the garage, located under the service road, to light and air.

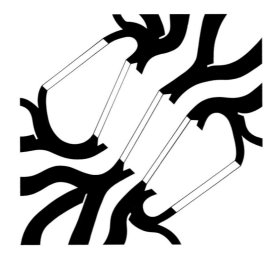
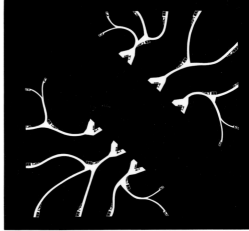
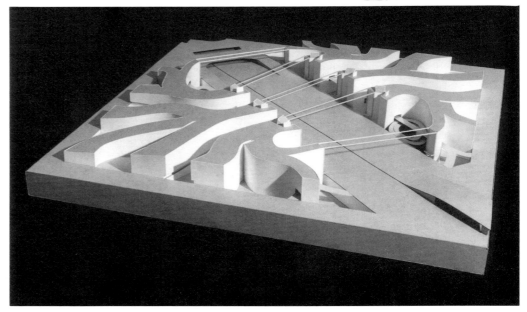

Texas at Arlington examines the highway as a new context which can stimulate new architectural responses. Rather than trying to reformulate the nature or patterning of the road itself, Price's investigations tackle the problem in architectural terms, seeking new building shapes with which to engage the highway. Drawing upon both artistic and natural analogies, these engagements form intense moments where the road and the architecture can be seen as extensions of one another, and old concepts of imageability and orientation can be reinterpreted in terms of the fluidic experience of the high speed highway.

While the design studies respond to specific contextural conditions in the Dallas–

132

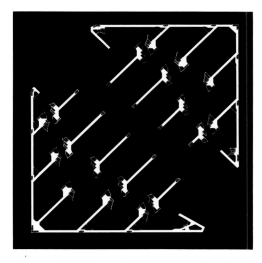

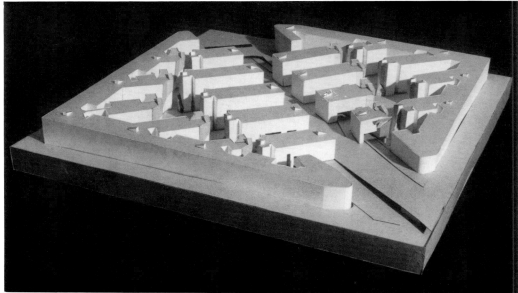

Fig. 10.2. Scheme II (Brian Powell and Dan Lyons) is based on a series of overlapping rhythms that begin as hard-edged, fingerlike forms along the high-speed freeway, cross the slow-speed service road, and finally erode and fracture into small-scale, linear segments forming the pedestrian zone. The building profile slopes from five to ten levels above the exterior level while the internal ground plane slopes in the reverse direction to maintain a constant ten levels of office space within.

Fort Worth area, they also form a growing collection of dynamic, typological "specimens"—similar to the comparative mapping of existing squares and other urban segments documented by Camillo Sitte in his 1889 book *Der Städtebau nach seinen Kunstlerichsen Grundsatzen* (translated into English as *The Art of Building Cities*[11] in 1945) and more recently by Rob Krier.[12]

The freeway offers less in the way of viable, whole examples for study than do the historical sections of cities. Instead the modern freeway presents the challenge of a vast array of dynamic contextural situations upon which to formulate the principles for new building typologies whose shape, position, and articulation can bring a sense of place to the wanderings of the modern road.

Architecture in the Landscape of the Highway
Martin Price
We need to begin by seeing the highway as a significant element of the landscape into which buildings are positioned; to engage the building with the linear, curvi-linear, rising and descending energies of the highway. We can create a powerful new source of creative energies by responding to the pulsating rhythm and beats, the speed of motion of the highway experience. An appropriate architecture would follow the principle of letting it flow: flowing lines, flowing spaces—flowing forms analogous to the flow of a river. This architecture can express a consonance with the highway by sculpturally scraping the land and by sculpturally stroking the sky to form broad panoramas of kinetic art.

Such an architecture must take as a given the moving point of view and the subsequent requirement that it will most often be viewed obliquely rather than frontally. The powers of this oblique view were understood by Alvar Aalto when he designed the Baker House dormitory at Massachusetts Institute of Technology with its undulating facade that emphasizes views up and down the Charles River.

Since the highway follows a predominantly horizontal vector, the architecture must also act in concert with the horizontal flow of force. The rhythms of the buildings can follow many forms: they can parallel the highway; run at a perpendicular to it; they can undulate and snake along the road; even bridge over and under it. Rhythm and interval can be used to organize the articulation of the buildings, with windows and other architectural features capturing a sense of dynamic motion—the musical beat of the highway. Scale and perspective can also be manipulated by the positioning of the building and by the variations in rhythm and intervals of the composing elements. Color can also be used to mirror the spectrum of colors of the vehicles traveling the road: ceramic tile or porcelain enameled panels provide limitless possibilities. Donald Judd's sculptures offer examples of how sequences of colored stripes can be used to dramatize the dynamics of motion.

The engagement of architecture with the highway can result in a more organic integration of forms and forces, perhaps in a way that is analogous to how rivers have carved glorious canyons in the Southwest. The possibility of flanking the sides of a highway with buildings and landscape stimulates an image of a canyon, perhaps enclosed by architectural cliffs and mesas. Whenever a roadway crosses a highway, the highway usually descends slightly to accommodate the crossing, thus exposing the earth berms on each side so that the sequence follows a series of rising and descending profiles. In a similar way, an architecture which interacts and joins with the highway can rise and fall to create a more natural unfolding and sky-stroking profile. Once the building has defined and played to the hard edge of the highway, it can respond with a softer and perhaps broken line as it moves away from the road, creating a precinct with the scale and rhythm of pedestrian movement.

The desired effort to have an architecture that poetically responds to the rivers of mechanical motion depends on overcoming two critical pollution problems. The first is an acoustical one, the intense noises and erratic vibrations which are pressures exerted by moving traffic. These can be effectively neutralized by making acoustical buffering a logical part of the criteria for freeway buildings rather than an afterthought. The second and more critical problem concerns the pollution of the air by the internal combustion engine — a problem that can only be solved by seeking less polluting alternatives. One has to be optimistic about solving this problem since our survival depends upon it.

Notes

1. Gyorgy Kepes, *The Nature and Art of Motion* (New York: George Braziller, 1965), i.

2. Gerald Holton, "Science and the Deallegorization of Motion," in Kepes, ed., *The Nature and Art of Motion,* 30–31.

3. Kepes, *The Nature and Art of Motion,* iv.

4. Donald Appleyard, "Motion, Sequence and the City," in Kepes, *The Nature and Art of Motion,* 176.

5. Ibid.

6. Donald Appleyard et al., *The View from the Road* (Cambridge: MIT Press, 1964).

7. Cf. Lawrence Halprin, *The RSVP Cycles* (New York: George Braziller, 1970).

8. Lawrence Halprin, *Freeways* (New York: Reinhold, 1966), 113–34.

9. Michel Foucault, "Space Knowledge and Power," in *The Foucault Reader* (Pantheon Books, 1984), 244.

10. Halprin, *Freeways,* 5.

11. (New York: Reinhold, 1945).

12. Rob Krier, *Urban Space* (London: Academy Editions, 1979).

Face to Face in the Center

William H. Whyte

I am going to talk about some minor phenomena of the city: schmoozing; girl watching; the rhythms of the interminable good-bye; reciprocal gestures. I do so to illustrate a properly serious thesis. It is this. The city has been undergoing a brutal restructuring; it has been losing people and jobs and many of its traditional functions. But the city has also been reasserting its most ancient function, as a central place where people come together—face to face.

No, say the skeptics. The city has had it. It will live on yes, still good for culture and that sort of thing. But the real action is out along the freeways. Here is the future. The towers of the office park are now the most striking elements of the new skylines. The center, in sum, has been split up and relocated to the periphery. No need for centrality. Advances in electronic communication have made obsolete the advantages of the center.

Valid?

Let's start with a look backward. Not so long ago the city was being excoriated for having too many people. It was bad and not because of faulty operation—traffic, air pollution, and such. It was bad because it was inherently so—structured to compress too many people in too little space. Experiments with rats and mice showed that crowding made them neurotic and suicidal. *Ergo,* cities are no damn good. "Behavioral sinks," that's what they were.

Television documentary films on the city went a step further; they generally opened with a shot of hell on earth: Fifth Avenue crowds, taken with a telephoto lens so that eight blocks seemed squeezed into one. The sound tracks featured sirens, jackhammers, a bit of discordant Gershwin. In one, as Fifth Avenue was faded out there was an arpeggio on the harp and a fade into a little child running up a hill in a new town.

Salvation? Yes. Documentaries would show hard hats with wrecking balls demolishing old buildings. (The hard hats were shown as the good guys! Preservationists were a small bunch of oddballs). As the dingy old downtowns were razed one saw the new city: clusters of high-rise projects set on podiums of concrete or grass.

We have come a very long way since. What has been taking place is a rediscovery of the city—on its own terms. We have been finding that it has its pleasures; that some of the old buildings give continuity and character; that the city isn't such a bad place to do business. It is not a utopian view; but it is a hopeful one.

Let me touch on it briefly from the perspective of our research. In the early 1970s I got some foundation grants to look at the city's streets and spaces and how people used them, or didn't use them. (One of the grants was from the National Geographic Society's Research Group. It was an "expedition grant," the first to be given for a domestic study.)

How many people was too many? What were the limits of crowding? The carrying capacity of an urban space? With direct observation and time-sequenced photography we studied people in a different kinds of everyday situations.

The first thing that struck us was the high frequency of chance encounters. People seemed to be running into friends and acquaintances at a fairly good clip. As we finally realized, the encounters weren't chance; they were a matter of actuarial probability. With a high number of people in a given area of downtown, the propinquity has its benefits as well as its disadvantages.

Another discovery was the "hundred-percent conversation." When people ran into each other on the street, how far would they move out of the pedestrian traffic stream to have their discussion? I had a splendid hypothesis: they would move to that strip of space alongside buildings, where people rarely walk. We charted all conversations lasting two minutes or longer (starting off at Fifty-third Street and Fifth Avenue in New York). To our surprise the people didn't move out of the traffic stream; if anything, they moved into it, and the longer the conversation, the more apt it was to be smack in the middle—in real estate parlance, the "hundred-percent location." Whatever people may say, what attracts them most in a city is other people. You see the same patterns in sitting. When people sit on the steps of a building, they feel comfortable there and if they block traffic a bit, no one seems to mind. But at places they don't like, they don't sit and block traffic.

The street is a great place for the prolonged good-bye. If you observe them long enough, you can learn to spot the false good-bye from the real one. Watch two men who can't say good-bye. The foot motions are the give-away. So is the look at the watch. Don't be taken in by it. It's only premonitory.

The best good-byes are those exchanged by executives as they break up after lunch. Or begin to. Now, at last, the real business of the lunch is brought up. The deal. There are all sorts of foot and body motions, and as the good-bye progresses, the motions become reciprocal; that is, after one man circles some 180 degrees to the right; another may follow, after some seconds, with a similar circling movement to the left. There is a symmetry to these rituals which bespeaks accommodation. The street serves them well. It is a fine place for striking deals. It is neutral territory, with neither party getting a locational edge. Like the chance encounter, it is one of the great benefits of the center of the city.

I have been citing examples of a trend towards the rediscovery of the city; to an appreciation of the basic role of the central marketplace. And the unifying element is the street. It is the city center's river of life. Now let us turn to the countertrend. Its underpinnings are ideological, but its effects eminently physical. Essentially, they involve the grafting of suburban forms on urban places and they would eliminate the most basic element of all—which brings us to the war against the street. It is being put up in second level walkways; down in subterranean concourses. It is being put everywhere but street level. Why?

Protection from the weather is one obvious reason. But that doesn't really explain it. Some of the most extensive systems are in cities with balmy climates. Conversely, some of the coldest, wintriest cities do very well without such protection. Another reason given is that perennial favorite, separation of vehicular and pedestrian traffic. This is supposed to be for the good of the pedestrian. It is no such thing. It is for vehicles. Look who gets the prime space: vehicles. They get the ground level; the pedestrian is sent up, or down, so that vehicles will have a clearer field. This contributes to another favorite, "relief from pedestrian congestion. This all-purpose cause is being invoked in almost every zoning measure for downtowns. Whatever it's about—sidewalks, roadways, atria, arcades, skyways, tunnels—the big benefit is "relief from pedestrian congestion."

What pedestrian congestion? What many of these cities badly need is pedestrian congestion. They have few enough people on the sidewalks as it is. To siphon off more by off-street systems robs downtown of the healthy flow that it ought to have. Dallas is an example. It has a fairly tight downtown, and an office workforce you would expect to produce very lively sidewalk flows. Not so. At midday the volumes are around 1500–1800 people per hour on the principal streets; quite low for such a high density downtown. Where are they all? Off the street. Down in the salad bars of the concourse; on the skyways; in the company cafeterias and in-house spaces liberally provided.

One of the appeals of such systems is newness; like high-tech, they promise a quantum leap and this is very important for cities with image problems, and for those that have lost their egos. Smaller cities are particularly vulnerable. They are the ones most immediately hit by the competition of the outlying malls; characteristically, they gear up for bold action about the time the last department store boards up its windows. From such cities go delegations in search of models. They go to Minneapolis and they are impressed with the skyways. They go to Montreal and they are impressed with Place Ville Marie and the underground concourses. So they go back home with visions of skyways and concourses.

What they do not go back with is the context that makes these things work. They do not go back with eighteen-below-zero temperatures; they do not go back with hundred-percent locations like those of the IDS Center or Place Ville Marie, nor with the very high densities that animate them. They go back to cities with low densities and hardly enough street life to sustain one level, let alone two or three.

The new one can kill off the old. There can be just so much business for downtown's retailers. If yet another level is added, something will have to give. Sometimes it is the new, additional level that bombs. But sometimes it is the street level. This is what has happened in Charlotte, North Carolina. A new, second-level complex of shops and walkways has been quite successful—so much so that it has become the dominant level. Middle-class whites are its constituency. Street level, with its bus stops, is given over primarily to blacks, lower income people, and people without cars.

The downward rating of street level is unplanned at first. But then a sort of Gresham's Law (gold v. paper money) sets in. If a city puts its bets on the off-streets, it has motive for downgrading the regular street. Minneapolis is an example. For a while there was a nice coexistence between its street retailing and its walkway system, but this is changing. A dullification process is under way. The most recent shopping complex is a huge box; save for a few windows, street level is solid, blank wall.

Such new complexes look like suburban shopping malls because they were meant to. Cities that have been badly hurt by malls sometimes adopt the if-you-can't-beat-'em-join-'em tactic and welcome malls to downtown. There is an apparently hardheaded reason for doing so. As one of the leading marketing consultants put it, the middle class will not come back to the city unless you provide them protection from the city. Thus the sealed box, the direct access by car. The ultimate step in this direction is the megastructure. These are big, usually requiring the demapping of a street. They enclose in one complex an office tower or two, a hotel, shopping concourses, and, inevitably, an atrium with greenery, fountains, and glass-walled elevators. The Bonaventure—ARCO complex in Los Angeles—is an outstanding example.

While there is an ideological basis to the fortress aspects, most of the design similarities are due to simple inertia. When developers of malls turn to the city, they usually take their architects and leasing people with them. What these people know is suburban shopping malls and that's what gets put up downtown. Hence the blank walls. Out in the malls they are functional. There's no need there for display windows to attract passersby. There are no passersby. People have already made the decision to enter by driving their car to the mall. In the city there are passersby and windows are quite functional. But the suburban form dominates. The same is often true of office buildings. Developers of suburban office parks tend to put up suburban office parks—clusters of towers set in a podium of grass. No retailing at street level either; leasing agents say it won't work.

Another push has come from incentive zoning. Increasingly, it has been bonusing developers away from the street, with the open space internalized within the buildings in the form of atria, arcades, "through-block circulation areas." This has been done in the name of the street—"to relieve pedestrian congestion." It was a misplaced emphasis and the planning commission recognized that something had gone wrong. As one of the consultants on a revamping of the zoning plan, I had the job of evaluating the various kinds of spaces that had been bonuses. Most of the spaces for "pedestrian circulation," I found, weren't used much. People liked the street better. We junked all the bonuses save for small parks.

One consequence of the shift to internal public spaces has been a shift in the public served. This was not at all the intent of the bonuses given for such spaces. They were to be true public spaces open to all comers. But there has been a subtle self-screening process, and in some cases not so subtle. To cite Minneapolis again, one of the nicest things about the IDS Crystal Court was the mixture of people. The seating in the middle attracted all sorts; in the morning there would be many older people. They didn't come to buy anything—most didn't have the money. They came to look at the other people, chat with acquaintances. They no longer have the possibility. New owners took over the building. They removed the public seating, keeping only the café seating.

Underground concourses are open to all comers and they are billed as fine environments in their own right. Proposals for the Dallas network sketched a place actually more amenable than the ground level above: "Amid the crowded office buildings lies a sheltered pedestrian mall. Its comfortably lighted, air-conditioned walkways are lined with attractive shops and dining places. . . The system will be a boon to tens of thousands of office workers, during lunch hour and in their twice daily walks between desk and parking place. For conventioneers, shoppers and other visitors it will offer an environment that is agreeable to be in, safe at all times, and protected from the elements and the noise and fumes of traffic."

So it is. So are others. But how well, really, do they stack up as environments? If proponents had to spend more time in their underground utopias, they would have second thoughts. These places are, for one thing, strangely disorienting. Stand in one place for a while and you will be accosted by people who have gotten lost and want to know where something is. The illuminated YOU ARE HERE signs don't help them much. Where, they wonder, is *here*? That is the problem. Here is a wall or set of pillars like other walls and sets of pillars. Designers compound the problem by their liking for symmetry. So North Corridor A is the mirror image of South Corridor B. Even the veteran gets turned around. There is a want of uniqueness. Nothing is askew, as it is topside; no steeple, no dome. There is no fixed point to sight on, no sky or sun.

Spaces which are not disorienting have some visual tie-in with the outside world. You can see out of them; you can see into them. Place Ville Marie in Montreal has a glassed entry at street level on one side; within, several small courts are open to the plaza and sky above. The IBM atrium in New York is transparent to the street on three sides.

But these are exceptions. Most of the internal spaces of megastructures have no tie-in with the street. Houston Center is a striking example. The whole thing is elevated up over the ground level. Where is ground level? One is confused. Renaissance Center has had similar problems. (The Project for Public Spaces in New York was retained to develop some solutions.) A new shopping center in Montreal, Les Terrasses, so confused customers with its many levels and half-levels that it had to be closed down for repairs and reworked. It still is confusing.

But perhaps the most disorienting thing about these off-street spaces is their deadly similarity. Where are you? An atrium by O'Hare Airport? Penn Center concourse in Philadelphia, Quakerbridge Mall? Regional cues are few. As a matter of fact, it's a question what country you're in. Japan? Yaesu Square in Tokyo? A center in the Paris suburbs? Everywhere is so alike: the *Ficus benjamina,* the gift shops, the piped-in music, the game arcades. It is the universal environment.

People get used to it. They get to like it, more's the pity. They especially like it if the alternative is no longer available or attractive. It's similar to the blue cheese dressing offered in salad bars. Once you get used to it, you lose your taste for the real thing.

Let me turn now to another aspect of the environment: its dynamic as a business center. People who believe it has lost its dynamic point to the departure of many corporations as evidence. How did the corporations fare? There have been few studies on this critical point, so I have conducted one. I have tracked the comparative performance of the major corporations that left New York City during or before the mid-seventies — and the corporations that did not leave. The moves had been the subject of much research. There were detailed pro and con rankings of site A vs. site B. Computer printouts gave weightings for key factors: costs;

transportation; quality of life—very big—quality of life for the employees.

The first thing I found out was that you didn't have to go through all that research. All you had to do was look in the telephone directory. Where did the boss live? That's where the company was going to go. I plotted the home location of the boss before the move was made. Of thirty-eight corporations that had moved out of New York City, thirty-one moved to a place close to the boss's home. Eight miles was the average distance. There was a particularly dense clustering in the Greenwich, Connecticut area, bounded by the three principal golf clubs.

The correlation between residence and office did not extend to employees in general, Westchester and Fairfield counties having the highest average house prices in the United States. Employees had to seek quality of life somewhere else. Sorry about that. One of the expectations of the corporations was that people would want to come out and see them. But it became quickly apparent that they didn't. One could see this in the visitors' parking lot—near empty most of the time. I asked an executive at one of the headquarters what they did about visitors. "We hire them," he said, explaining that they booked their consultants to come out and see them more often.

In 1976 not enough time had elapsed for a fair measure of comparative performance. A decade later it had (I extended this to eleven years—for example, December 31, 1976 through December 31, 1987). The results were downright startling. Of the thirty-eight corporations that had relocated in suburbia, about a third had lost their identity through merger or acquisition. For the remaining twenty-four, the average increase in market value was 108 percent; the median 89 percent. (The Dow Jones industrial average for same period increased 99 percent.) Average increase for the thirty-nine which stayed in New York City: 288 percent.

How come? There are many possible explanations. But there is one that is paramount: the center is the center is the center. What the companies that stayed here have *not* cut themselves off from is the gossip of the Rialto, the cross-roads position; the chance encounter.

The new growth areas *look* like centers. Some look more like cities than the central one—Las Colinas instead of Dallas; the Fairfax County office parks outside Washington; Route 1 outside Princeton; Valley Forge beyond Philadelphia. They have upstaged the city. These places are expanding rapidly and there is no question they are siphoning away office work that had been the province of the city. It hurts to lose all those back-office jobs. New office facilities would make more sense within the city limits, city protagonists argue, and the transportation is already in place for them. But the outward trend continues. Since there is no mass transit to speak of, the car is dominant and the traffic jams are fierce. But this has not curbed the growth.

These outlying complexes, however, are not going to supplant the center. They will service it with computer and clerical functions; they will provide branch offices and regional headquarters. But they will not become the new cities of the future. Office parks, no matter how big, do not a city make. They lack centrality, and they lack it within their boundaries too. They do not integrate a series of related functions. They are a bunch of isolated components—office buildings, parking lots (huge parking lots)—and concrete cloverleafs and access roads. In most of them you don't walk. You'd be crazy to. Rarely are there sidewalks. Very functionless, this lack; interviews indicate that the kind of recreation most favored is walking—if there is a place for it. Ordinarily, however, it is considered very odd behavior. (I once walked all the mile and a half from Princeton to the Carnegie Center office complex, one of the very best. My arrival was greeted with incredulity, cheers, and a scolding.)

To come back to the question: Which way?

Megastructures are still being built, but there are signs that, as has been the way with forms of transportation, they have reached their peak of elaborateness after obsolescence has set in. The hotel John Portman designed for Times Square has just opened. But it was conceived some fifteen years ago; today it is an exhibit of clichés of the early 1970s, frozen in time, like some prehistoric mammoth.

The economic rationale for megastructures and fortresses never did make good sense. If people are seeking protection from the city, the city is a poor place for it. Better they stay away. But it appears that people do not come to the city for security. The places that base their appeal on security have not been doing so very well. Some, like Renaissance Center, have faced bankruptcy. By contrast, the most successful places have been ones abundantly and attractively open to the city. The Faneuil Hall Marketplace is virtually a celebration of the street; and it is doing more business than any other marketplace in the country.

Agora is a word loosely used these days. But if we look back to early Greece we find some parallels worth thinking about. In *How the Greeks Built Cities* (London, 1949), Wycherley tells us how the agora started out as a very simple place; in the center of things; some open space, some tables; a little bit later, some colonnades. Eventually, some cities moved the agora away from the center; later yet, they put a wall around it; then a complete structure. This coincided with the start of the decline of the cities.

Let me recapitulate. The city has been going through a brutal simplification. It has been losing functions for which it is no longer competitive: manufacturing has left; back-office workforces are moving to suburbia; the computers are already there. But as the city has lost some functions, it has been reaffirming its most basic one: that of the central marketplace. Thus, the great importance of a place to sit, trees to sit under, a passing parade to look at, sunlight unobstructed, chance encounters. Anything that makes this human congress easier, more spontaneous, more pleasant is at the heart of the most ancient function of the city: a place where people come together.

Face to face.

In the Landscape between Innocence and Experience
Malcolm Quantrill

12

While we were exploring some of the notions of "urban forms and suburban dreams," Bruce Webb suggested that the banner "Places between Here and There" might best describe our search for ways of place-making today. This suggestion has a haunting, mysterious quality, because it implies in this "between" a notion of travel and movement, rather than arrival and settlement. After all, if our search is conducted from a constantly shifting position, if the places we seek are not located, not locations at all, how can we arrive at them? If places themselves are in a "between" state, then the concepts of "being in place," "arriving at a place," the whole notion of "settlement," seem literally to have become *dis*placed.

Settlement implies gathering, a gathering together of ideas and memories expressed in things—demarcations of land, trees, walls, monuments, buildings. Within the settlement we find the context for Aldo Rossi's permanence.[1] There are particular places to gather, and we gather there to celebrate the existence of place, of special events. But in a permanent state of *between,* how can we focus on gathering? The rolling stone gathers no moss, as we know. Motion and gathering are opposed to each other. So, perhaps "places between here and there" are no places at all. And this might help explain our dilemma of place-making today.

But perhaps this is an oversimplification, too. Because, even if we do not gather moss as we travel, we certainly take our baggage with us. And this means we don't travel empty-handed—or rather, empty-minded. For when we are in this between state we are aware of where we have been and where we would like to go. We have our experiences of places we have known, and our imaginations are fed by the media. So, our expectations of places we might encounter and "settle for" are outlined by knowledge or the temptation of further knowledge. We are literally bombarded by images of what has been and what might be in our journey between here and there.

When we look at patterns of development in cities and suburbs over the past quarter-century, what we see must depend upon "where we are coming from."

Fig. 12.1. Professor Peter Faller looks down from the balcony of his duplex apartment in Der Wohnhügel ("Living Hill"), Neugereut, Stuttgart, Germany.

Our perception of the built environment is conditioned by the roads we have traveled, by the ways in which we have been conditioned. In other words, we do not have an innocent eye in viewing these things. What we seek, and what we see, will result from our exposure to ideas about the city, about architecture, the built framework, the cultural and commercial milieu in which we live, or in which we desire (or are persuaded we should desire) to live and work. Some of these ideas may come from experience of the "real thing," from which we have drawn valid knowledge of how we respond to and function in these environments. But some of our conditioning will come from the media, from scenarios constructed by those professionally skilled in selling environments. Different utopias are designed to be sold to particular social groups. As Burdette Keeland has observed: "You won't find either the intellectuals or the peasants in The Woodlands, Texas or other planned communities" (*Cite,* Houston, Spring, 1990).

Under such conditions, conditioned as we are, what can we make of these "places between here and there"? No longer innocent, are we yet sufficiently experienced in differentiating between the actual world and the media scenario to make constructive choices? Indeed, what can we construct in such circumstances? Our choices may well be very limited, and be choices only in the terms we have been conditioned to accept. Are we not, in fact, all of us caught "between here and there"? But perhaps there is also a positive side to this nonfixed place, because its lack of finite form also facilitates transmutation. Viewed from a constantly shifting position, it is also a natural agent of change.

Because places between here and there are not in a fixed state of being, they express a metamorphic freedom. They are stratified (Bakhtin) or subject to a continuous process of change and redefinition. Clearly, we cannot define a something or somewhere that is subject to such redefinition. It cannot have clear boundaries. If, on the other hand, we can understand architecture and environment as a dialogical process, in which certain "voices" emerge and present events, then this dialog can offer references of identity against which redefinition proceeds.

Texas is as good a place as any to study urban and suburban patterns of development. Houston, for example, in spite of two congregations of commercial monuments, does not display the characteristics of conventional urbanity: rather it is a collection of largely unrelated suburbs. Of so-called cities in Texas, only the state capital of Austin and the largely Hispanic San Antonio retain traditional urban forms in their centers. On the other hand, characteristic of the new *contra*urbs, is the suburban type community that is based not upon a city center but on the campus of a university, which stands in for a daytime city. Frequently, the structure of contraurbs, lacking a true urban center, quickly dissolves on its edges into the character of its rural surroundings.

The physical structure of contraurbs, just like that of typical suburbs in the United States, is essentially horizontal. This horizontal dimension if both promoted and extended by the automobile. Highways and roads provide convenient connections between the garage and the supermarket or workplace, and back again. The spaces and places between these points of departure and arrival are usually featureless. Indeed, even those points of departure and arrival are typically nonevents. We depart and return to the garage door, the *back* door to our house. The ritual and function of a front door, a significant point of personal entry that addresses both the street and the visitor, has become outmoded. Perhaps a few badly proportioned classical columns here and there may serve as a reminder of times past, but in reality the suburban architectural image is determinedly faceless. The significance of spaces and places, a sense of individuality or uniqueness, distinguishing marks in the landscape, these signs are not common in suburban form. This loss of image and identity is only partially attributable to the automobile, to speed of movement between places and the convenience of the back door into the house, the mall or the store. The missing dimension is also one of investment: but significantly that requires not only investment in Deutschmarks or dollars but also an investment of imagination and a concern for enrichment of experience rather than mere visual embellishment. Are the suburbs then unloved? They most certainly are not!

In fact, many people choose the suburban life-style because it has less crime and violence, because it provides a quiet and unharassing mode of life; and some would even say that suburbs generate a better sense of community. In reality, the horizontal spread of suburbs mitigates against social proximity and interaction. Street conversations with neighbors are typically more characteristic of Houston than they are of the suburbs. A friendly toot on a car horn often passes for a neighborly chat in suburbs and contraurbs. Horizontal spread simplifies both the architectural form and the social pattern. Suburbs are more like traditional villages, especially the Austrian *Langedorf* type, than like cities, yet they lack the social magnets of the traditional village. Although it is undeniably a great convenience, the automobile has diluted both the complexity of the architectural stage and the social drama enacted upon it. Apart from shopping and going to church, there is little to do in suburbia. As a consequence the gardens are loved, or at least dutifully manicured, and the golf course also comes in for a great deal of affection.[2] Like villages our modern suburbs are earth-rooted; indeed, the history of the suburban movement since the end of the nienteenth century has been centered on the acquisition of garden space, and it was from this kind of suburban ambition that the garden city movement grew. So, the garden, a notion of generous green open space, is an essential component of residential suburbia's image of itself. From that viewpoint the suburb might be seen as a backward-looking representation of modern reality, if not being exactly nostalgic in its attachment to historical examples of architectural form.

What, then, are the architectural and cultural issues generated by suburban and contraurban patterns, by the nonspecific representation of their form and character as "no-place"? Perhaps Karsten Harries's opening observations in his dialog with Christian Norberg-Schulz at the inaugural CASA symposium (1989)[3] provide a useful starting point. Harries said:
Let me refer to the famous temple passage in "The Origin of the Work of

Art," where Heidegger speaks of the temple-work as establishing a world and presenting the earth.

Heidegger's example suggests a possibility for architecture as possessing a strong ethical function, giving us a coherent world understanding and placing us firmly on the earth. In context Heidegger makes it quite clear that such temple-work lies behind us. It belongs to a past from which we are separated, not only by the obvious years, but more importantly by the shape of our modern world. So the question is, can this kind of work, moving as it is, illuminate our practice today any more than, let's say, my examples of farmhouses or Heidegger's Black Forest farmhouse?[4]

In this question to Norberg-Schulz, Harries is raising the problem of our present-day separation from the past and therefore from connections which have previously existed between building forms and the rituals that generated them. And he implies that we cannot respond today, in our separated and disconnected world, to the rituals that generated those earlier responses, for example, "the temple." In answering Harries, Norberg-Schulz stressed that Heidegger is not advocating a nostalgic return to earlier forms but to "a second beginning." This rebeginning is not, Norberg-Schulz reminds us, a restarting from point zero, but from a position of "guarding what we already know" and of "taking care of what we understand from the first beginning." Such an approach allows us to see architectural history not just as the evolution of things, but also as a resource of human experience, technical knowledge and cultural attitudes.

I recently asked my students to identify cultural archetypes in the changing architectural milieu of Texas. We soon agreed that the adventurous and rough-riding romance of the old frontier was still represented by the House of Pleasure, commonly known as the whorehouse, as evidenced by the advent of the popular musical *The Best Little Whorehouse in Texas.* The temple then emerged as the logical counterbalance to moral laxity and promiscuity, with the Catholic church and Baptist chapel continuing to coexist as essential centers of modern Texas life. With the moral issues taken care of, and the houses of sin and redemption identified as archetypes, we went on to ask what lay beyond the prospects of everyday temptations and reality. Education was our main hope, we decided, and the library seemed to suggest itself as the natural gateway to wisdom and advancement beyond immediate gratification and sorrow.

Suburbia, with its extended horizontal structure, is too simplistic to accommodate layers of complexity, diversity, and secrecy. Both temple and library can retain an archetypal form and assert their presence in the horizontal suburban sprawl. In a sea of nondescript houses the House of God and the House of Wisdom can bring to the architectural object or "thing" an *extraordinariness,* a particularity of *presence* and *spirit.* While both temple and library provide points of emphasis in the suburbs, the house of pleasure has no place to hide there. Within the suburban framework it could only be camouflaged by adopting one of its common urban conventions—by representing itself as an ordinary house. In other words, any house might be the whorehouse in suburbia, an option already explored by Giles Cooper in his play *Everything in the Garden.* Cooper depicts a bunch of bored suburban housewives, who allow themselves to be recruited by a London madam in an effort to overcome their boredom and supplement their pocket money.

The house of pleasure is a private place; you do not expect to meet your friends and neighbors there. In reality, in the modern suburbs the house of pleasure has largely been displaced by the health club, which might be called the House of Torture and commonly takes on the same appearance as the supermarket, complete with capacious parking lot.

The temple represents the idea of congregation, a coming together, a gathering as around the primeval hearth, a family united around the dining table as in the early Christian Church. As a focus of this ritual gathering it is both a public and a private place. It is a place set apart, a special place with which those who congregate there can identify; and it has, in turn, its own particular identity or *genius loci.*

A library, on the other hand, is a storehouse of knowledge. It is a special kind of storehouse, of course, but a storehouse nevertheless. The congregation of a library is its books. We go there not to congregate, as in the temple, but to select items from the shelves of the storehouse and then isolate ourselves with those resources of intellectual nourishment. I have spoken of Alvar Aalto's library at Viipuri as "an invitation to read,"[5] in an attempt to describe the modernity of Aalto's open, well-lit concept for the library interior.

Within a library knowledge is memorialized and the thirst for it is stimulated. As a building volume, however, the library remains essentially a storehouse, basically a shed. Andrew Carnegie must have been aware of this problem in endorsing the appearance of the Carnegie libraries as temples of knowledge. The modern, nonclassical library has abandoned the temple image. It contrasts with the supermarket mainly in the fact that its products are free and more diverse. Just as the supermarket requires its parking lot so, in order to give the modern library an *extraordinariness,* it is necessary to provide an extension of the "object," of the *thing* itself. At Viipuri, on the revised site where Aalto built his library in 1933, he had the advantage of the city's Torkkeli Park to establish this distinctive quality.

As we have already observed, the garden or open green space belongs just as much to suburbia and contraurbia as to the city proper. In the city, of course, we expect a grandeur of scale and occasion in our parks. This is consistent not only with the large population that uses its recreational focus, but also with the rituals of equestrian exercise, concerts around the open-air bandstand, ice-skating, and

Fig. 12.2. Apartment complex, Old People's Home, Neugereut, Stuttgart—exterior from approach, illustrating a sense of place.

special celebrations and processions. The great city parks, having been established for two or three hundred years, have huge old trees and other memories beyond momentary festivities. Greenwich park, on the south bank of the River Thames, with its queen's house (Inigo Jones), Royal Naval Hospital (Christopher Wren), and Observatory (John Vanburgh) is an excellent example of landscaped urbanity. But in the suburbs, too, the park can create a special place, an oasis in the suburban desert: a public garden.

When we look at the character of suburbia and the potential for contraurbia the element of the garden, the green open space, is clearly a prerequisite. Of equal weight, it would appear, are the street, the parking lot, the supermarket, the cultural shed and, of course, the temple. The essential struggle in the suburbs is between street and garden, between tarmac and grass. All other suburban conflicts are of a lesser degree. But the parking lot aggressively assumes a dominant role in the *Zwischenraum* between traveling and arriving. This is most clearly observable in the case of the supermarket. If the library were as much in demand as the general store, then the parking lot would also dominate the approach to the library.

Before the advent of the automobile it was taken for granted that we might be rained on when arriving at or leaving a building. The *porte-cochère* is our best guarantee of staying dry. A parking lot in close proximity to the building is, at best, only second best. In the battle between automobile and architecture the parking lot will inevitably assume a dominant role over the buildings—especially in the prevailing horizontality of the suburbs—whenever there are not clear priorities in the signification of the one versus the other. The signification of the supermarket is typically vested in a company label or product symbol—we are now learning to recognize Apple Tree as a substitute for Safeway. A combination of this label and an extensive parking lot spells SUPERMARKET. Community and civic facilities, such as temple and library, are not dependent upon this commercial coding. In the case of the house of God and the house of wisdom there is, arguably, a value above and beyond utilitarian convenience. The ubiquitous parking lot is not, at the same time, a universal signal. Differentiation in approach, appearance, and experience remains as an option between commercial and cultural life. If there is not such differentiation then the two-dimensionality of suburbia is even further flattened out.

The planning and realization of a new Episcopal church in Texas revealed this characteristic struggle between the identity of building form and the dominance of the parking element. Before setting out on the design of their new church, the parish priest and his planning committee made a tour of Catholic, Episcopal and Lutheran churches recently built in Texas. The parishioners wanted to identify the quality of *churchness* that came closest to their own ambitions, and hoped, in the process, also to identify an architect with whom they could work.

Early in the debate between the church planning committee and the original architect, the battle lines that dictated the hierarchy of parking and building were clearly drawn. It was argued by a majority of committee members that the visibility of the parking lot on approach to the church was essential as a magnet for the congregation. This argument could not be substantiated by facts. The congregation for the new church would be thoroughly established prior to the construction of the new building. At the time of the planning process the new congregation was already meeting in a local elementary school. By the time the new building was completed at least three-quarters of the ultimate size of the congregation for the new parish would be formed. The parishioners would, therefore, know where to park when they arrived at the new church. Although the congregation would probably grow by a further twenty-five percent over the next five to ten years, the possibility of casual, out-of-town worshippers driving to the somewhat remote suburban site was extremely unlikely. In the event that some such casual visitors were searching for this particular church, they would certainly be looking for a distinctive building rather than place to park.

Although there was general agreement, therefore, that it was the building form rather than the parking facility that would signal *church,* committee members ultimately had little faith in the architectural symbol of their belief and the architect was instructed "to achieve a proper balance between the building and the means of access and parking." As a result all the earlier discussion of the characteristics of (1) "arrival at a special, blessed place," and (2) "the creation of a garden environment at the point of approach that will impart the spirit of St. Francis of Assisi" with emphasis on (3) "a sense of the monastic cloister which will ensure a clear detachment of this place of worship from the busy outer world," was set aside to give vehicular approach and parking places precedence over the architectural form and experience of the church itself. Heidegger's sense of "guarding what we already know" and "taking care of what we understand from the first beginning" was therefore lost by both the planning committee and the architect early in the design process.[6]

There was an obvious failure to understand that a church in the suburbs needs more rather than less emphasis: that a sense of *genius loci* and a particularity of place and experience is essential to distinguish the house of worship from the warehouse or the undistinguishable house of pleasure. The result is the loss of any particular identity of the architectural object, the church: for while the *thing* itself is there, its sense of extraordinariness—what Marco Frascari calls "the sense of wonder"[7]—has not been exploited or developed. Although there was a good understanding of the potential of St. Francis church to be a true landmark in the suburbs, and a thoroughly democratic discussion of the principles by which this could be achieved had taken place, the necessary investment of imagination had not, in the final analysis, been made.

Architecture bridges the known and the unknown; it is between the "real" and the "virtual" worlds, when this unknown dimension finds expression in architecture, that we experience it as more than mere form. Architectural extraordinariness is, above all, the celebration and memorialization of an imagination that transforms an ordinary event of space and form into a special experience so that we are, in Frascari's terms, "stunned" by it. And the suburbs and contraurbs are crying out for such astonishing experiences.

Making a mark in the suburban desert, creating a landmark in what I have called the underground skyline[8] of suburban form, requires the identification of, and adherence to, a number of fundamental principles. These concern the notion of a place and the ways in which the features of that place give it a particular identity. This process of identification is of special importance in the case of a suburban site, where there may be no natural features to give us a clue about this identity of place. If there are no *things* already on the site—no trees, no distinctive rock or earth formations, no water—then the process of introducing things requires particular sensitivity and skill. In this case the things we import into a featureless place are truly artificial, man-made artifacts, and the process by which they are invented and orchestrated may be accurately described as *artifice*.

Establishing an identity for a suburban site is therefore a process just as complex as that of dealing with a similar problem in the city. In addition, the process is often more difficult, yet little effort has been made to understand it. For example, the placing of a tower in the city in relation to other adjacent building masses of lower profile may give a building or site a special significance. Although a tower may provide the basis for a suburban landmark, however, it would not alone give identity to an isolated site. Without the advantage of limiting boundaries, the effect of a tower in helping delineate the character of a site is not as comprehensive; it is not site-specific. In establishing the identity of the suburban site, therefore, all the imported elements must be invented and orchestrated with artifice. A single architectural gesture is not enough when there is no framework to receive this flourish, or no background against which we can read it. In the same way, and this has special reference to the relationship between the form of the building and the parking lot, the placing of the building in a particular part of the site is not in itself a sufficient gesture.

Louis Kahn posed the significant question: "What does the building want to be?" In approaching the design of a suburban site we must consider also the question: "What does this place want to be?" In other words: "What is the suburban site's ambition for itself?" When we truly develop a site—not just in the commercial sense of realizing a plot ratio in terms of the optimum number of square feet— our aim should be to realize its potential as the *place* of temple or library by dreaming a dream for that site. This is the role of imagination: that is the purpose of human artifice when we make signs.

Imagine, therefore, a treeless and featureless site on the northern outskirts of Austin, on which a Catholic priest has to create his new parish church of Albertus Magnus. Certainly, he wants his church to send out a signal of its existence. But he also wants to generate messages within the site for those who come to pray and worship there. The priest has a wish list of the things he wants to achieve. But he is not experienced in imagining a whole environment to accommodate his wishes. He needs help in translating his list of wishes into a coherent whole, a total religious experience for the congregation. His site is a dreary piece of suburban real estate. How can we breathe an atmosphere into this nonplace, creating an extraordinary place, a sense of wonder in a nowhere? We can make a start by asking what this place could be, by suggesting metaphors that would transform noplace into a special and unique place.[9]

For instance, taking the precedent discussed in approaching the design of the new Episcopal church for Texas, does the site want to be a garden or a woodland park? Perhaps this Austin site was once covered with trees. It might take time, but would it be helpful if this woodland past were recreated in a future dream? This would be one way of establishing the site boundaries, by creating an oasis in the middle of the suburban desert. If we planned to make a woodland park, then we could cut "clearings" into it, creating a number of *templa,*[10] making a pattern of such spaces into which to insert the church, the outdoor processional way, the tower, a shrine—all the wishes on the parish priest's list—and, of course, the parking lot sheltered and hidden by the trees.[11]

There are other metaphors we could adopt, other precedents we could follow. For example, we might reserve the woodland park for the parking lot and concentrate attention on the use of the built form to create the overall *genius loci.* This would involve heavy dependence upon the notion of grouping the buildings to provide an entrance court or cloister, creating a distinction between an outer world and an inner world within the site boundaries. In such a metaphor, the church, chapel or shrine, tower, social and educational facilities, and the presbytery would frame the experiences of this special place, and the emphasis of established architectural precedents would therefore be greater. The effect would be to give more sense of urbanity to the suburban site, although the experience of passing from one space to another would be on a smaller scale. This problem of transforming monastic scale to reduced circumstances is a difficulty when adopting such a precedent for a new suburban church.

An alternative to the dense urban character of the monastic model would be that of the traditional walled parish church of central and northern Europe, where both church and tower are set in a graveyard that is framed by an enclosing wall. This village model is usually entered through a formal gateway, and often sits in a rather open landscape. When I ventured out of the medieval city of Norwich as a young child, this was the first church type to impinge on my consciousness.

In contrast, we might dream of a transformation of site topology by literally submerging the built forms and creating what Reima Pietilä calls "land*shape* architecture."[12] This metaphor, like that of the woodland park, returns the site to an *other* nature, a natural form such as it might once have had. In this case the undulation of the site's built forms would provide the landmark characteristics and the convention of a church tower would be out of character and superfluous.

Another metaphor drawn from my Finnish experience concerns the work of Alvar Aalto, and in particular those of his buildings I have described as his "urban fragments."[13] Aalto's urban fragments are buildings conceived not as self-important monuments, but as component parts of an urban environment to which they bring a sense of the city in miniature — a piazza or courtyard, for example, that establishes a sense of place within an essentially anonymous building mass. Examples of this are Säynätsalo Town Hall, the National Pensions Institute in Helsinki, and Rautatalo (Iron House), also in Helsinki. The use of the urban fragment in the suburbs is another means of establishing a sense of place in suburban "noplace," using this *other* thing (urban fragment) to create a particular quality and effect.

In the case of these four metaphors, the emphasis is on achieving a transformation of the existing featureless site into a special place that has the distinctive characteristics of woodland, or a land formation or urban architectural place. We might note that the Franciscan Order, in colonizing North and Central America, prepared standardized church designs, with a range of size and form that could be adapted to any basically flat site. But the principle proposed in the metaphor approach for fulfilling suburban site potential is not intended to standardize environments or experiences. In fact, even the standardized Franciscan church designs permitted considerable variation in the built forms. Certainly, the metaphor approach to structuring artifice in suburban site design is proposed in opposition to the so-called "topological" method of school design in New York State, which advocates a standard plan arrangement that may be expanded or contracted to fit any site. Central to the notion of the metaphoric approach to artifice, to the process of orchestrating *things,* is the act of creating "voices" that can speak to us in generating the essential dialog of place-making.

The history of architecture shows us that the value of precedent and the standardization of plan form and construction is in the variety of effect that can be achieved in interpretation and transformation. This is the situation in which we still find ourselves in our *landschaft zwischen unkenntnis und erlebnis* (landscape between ignorance and understanding). The suburban site is never entirely innocent and our approach to it should therefore not flirt with any sham innocence.

Architecture represents the accumulated experience of human efforts in celebrating and memorializing place and space. By generating a sense of extraordinari-

Fig. 12.4. Apartment complex, Old People's Home, Neugereut, Stuttgart—interior solar atrium, with tropical plants, to give the impression of a Mediterranean vacation resort hotel.

Malcolm Quantrill

ness from standardized things, by harnessing the experience embodied in established precedents to overcome innocence and naivete, architecture has continually built bridges between historical pasts and our present predicament. That is the meaning of architecture—*our experience of artifice in action.* Protesting our innocence of this fact is comparable to denying a birthright. It is a component that we should be building into our whole educational system, not just the education of architects.

We understand that our suburbs are a collection of things, but we should question what these things add up to. The aggregation of *somethings* makes up the city and provides the physical framework of civilization. Nothings cannot add up to anything but noplace. Venturi's distinction between the "duck" and the "painted shed" may describe the basic options of the suburban strip.[14] But to imagine that a painted shed can achieve the complex identity of the St. Mark's Basilica in Venice without the investment of many generations of memories is to deny the whole process of culture and of architecture itself.

Architecture is not at all like fast food. It is more like Fabianism, which was founded on "the inevitability of gradualness." The very continuity of architecture demands that it is constantly being reformed and revised, with different bits being added and taken away. It is by this constant caressing that the *thing* is loved into lasting life. Its special quality comes from our affection for those things we gather to make a special place, an *extraordinary* experience. This *erlebnis*—understanding—is essential to what we must aspire to in the regrounding of architecture,[15] grounding it truly in the foundations of experience; abandoning the confused state and esthetic of no-man's-land of ignorance—*unkenntnis*.

Notes

The foregoing was originally given as a lecture in honor of Professor Antero Markelin on the occasion of his sixtieth birthday, at Das Institut für Stadtsplannung, Technische Universität, Stuttgart, May 9, 1991.

1. Aldo Rossi, *The Architecture of the City* (Cambridge: MIT Press, 1982).

2. Amos Rapoport, *The Meaning of the Built Environment: A Non-verbal Communication Approach* (Berkeley Hills, Calif.: Sage, 1982), 129–30.

3. "Constancy and Change in Architecture" was the theme of the inaugural Center for the Advancement of Studies in Architecture (CASA) International Symposium held at the College of Architecture, Texas A&M University, April 12–14, 1989, in collaboration with the University of Houston and the Brochstein Foundation (Houston), and in honor of Professor Christian Norberg-Schulz of Oslo, Norway, who was the principal speaker.

4. Malcolm Quantrill and Bruce Webb, eds., *Constancy and Change in Architecture*

(College Station: Texas A&M University Press, 1991), 61.

5. Malcolm Quantrill, *Alvar Aalto: A Critical Study* (London and New York: Schocken, 1983), 63.

6. Personal notes from the Planning Committee of the Episcopal Church of St. Francis, College Station, Texas, 1985–86.

7. See Marco Frascari, "A Wonder of the *City Beautiful* Surburbia: The *Mirabilis Suburbis* of Coral Gables, Miami," this volume.

8. Malcolm Quantrill, *The Environmental Memory: Man and Architecture in the Landscape of Ideas* (New York: Schocken, 1987), 182–89.

9. Malcolm Quantrill, "A Studio Encounter," *Texture,* Texas A&M University, 1987, 5–6.

10. A concept of Ernst Cassirer, quoted by Michael Graves in *Representation and Architecture,* Akin and Weinel, eds.

11. Quantrill, "A Studio Encounter."

12. Malcolm Quantrill, *Reima Pietilä: One*

Man's Odyssey in Search of Finnish Architecture (Helsinki: 1988). See also the work of Martin Price, architect, professor at the University of Texas at Arlington.

13. Malcolm Quantrill, *The Environmental Memory: Man and Architecture in the Landscape of Ideas* (New York: Schocken, 1986), chapter 8, "Aalto's Use of Memory: The 'Urban Fragments.'"

14. Robert Venturi, *Complexity and Contradiction in Architecture* (New York: Museum of Modern Art, 1967).

15. At the editorial board meeting following the inaugural CASA symposium, the decision was made to reground debate in the *Grundfragen* of architecture. See Stanford Anderson, "Regrounding Architecture," in Quantrill and Webb, *Constancy and Change in Architecture,* 147–49.